T0413355

Human-Centered Management

Five Pillars of Organizational Quality
and Global Sustainability

HUMAN
CENTERED
MANAGEMENT

5 Pillars of **Organizational Quality**
and **Global Sustainability**

Maria-Teresa Lepeley

Greenleaf
PUBLISHING

Published by Greenleaf Publishing Limited
Salts Mill, Victoria Road, Saltaire, BD18 3LA, UK
www.greenleaf-publishing.com

The right of Maria-Teresa Lepeley to be identified as Author of this Work has been asserted by her in accordance with sections 77 and 78 of the Copyright, Designs and Patents Act 1988.

Cover by Sadie Gornall-Jones

Printed and bound by Printondemand-worldwide.com, UK

British Library Cataloguing in Publication Data:
    A catalogue record for this book is available from the British Library.

    ISBN-13: 978-1-78353-789-1 [hardback]
    ISBN-13: 978-1-78353-790-7 [paperback]
    ISBN-13: 978-1-78353-796-9 [PDF ebook]
    ISBN-13: 978-1-78353-788-4 [ePub ebook]

To my grandchildren Lucas (12), Augustin (11), Camila (10), Adriana (9), and Antonela (7) from whom I have learned more and faster than my grandmothers learned from me.

Contents

PART III HUMAN-CENTERED MANAGEMENT AND SUSTAINABLE QUALITY (SQ)

Figures and tables

Figures

Tables

Box

Preface

Change is a constant of our time. It is imminent, unavoidable, and pressing organizations locally and globally to find new ways to do things with resilience, agility, and the quality standards required to become sustainable. The unprecedented speed, scale, and scope of change affects all organizations in the global VUCA (volatile, uncertain, complex, ambiguous) environment and is transforming the way people live, learn, work, and relate to one another.

How can people manage change effectively and how can organizations adapt to constant disruptions in the 21st century? These are questions that prompted me to research the subject and write this book aiming to optimize benefits for people and organizations. The book is based on three decades observing organization development, performance, and productivity with the end goal to become sustainable in an increasingly competitive global economy. I unveil how the development of National Quality Award programs in developed countries and a growing number of developing countries is providing significant support to an elite group of organizations reaching quality standards and excellence. And I highlight growing evidence showing that in spite of this very positive step forwards, many challenges remain to open access to quality standards for all organizations pursuing sustainability across industries and countries. In this demanding environment education and training have a critical responsibility. This book is a guide in this direction.

I titled this book—and the book series—*Human-Centered Management* to make clear that people are the *engine* of organizations, the economy, and inclusive societies built on foundations that encompass **affectiveness, effectiveness,** and **efficiency** (in this order). The book explains this emerging paradigm.

I have observed and dealt with change in organizations, the economy, and societies in developed and developing countries. And I need to emphasize that although I have never been afraid of change, because experience has consistently shown me that change is necessary for continuous improvement and sustainability, I am always challenged to identify new ways to innovate to overcome obstacles and solve barriers embedded in obsolescence. Along the way I have been fortunate to find creative, innovative, and visionary people who have stimulated me to expand knowledge to conquer new dilemmas. They are too many to mention and I would be at risk of omitting names in this limited space. I am grateful to all of them. I would not have written this book or edited this HCM book series if they had not crossed my global path.

Maria-Teresa Lepeley
October 2016
Winter Park, Florida

The book at a glance

Human-Centered Management: The 5 Pillars of Organization Quality and Sustainability

Organizations	HC Management	HC SQ Management
Structure: *(hardware)*	1. Human Capital	5. Sustainable Quality Model
Mission, vision, values, identity, planning	2. Disruption Resilience	- 7 Management Areas
Teamwork (long term)		- 35 Assessment Elements
Strategies: *(software)*	3. Talent Management	Quality Cycle & Scoring:
Change, innovation		- *performance evaluation*
Networks (short term)	4. Agility	- *continuous improvement*
		- *sustainable quality*

Part I

Why Human-Centered Management?

1

A long-overdue
paradigm shift

We live among global disruptions that require constant organization innovation (Maria-Teresa Lepeley)

The 2015–2016 Global Competitiveness Report has been
launched at a pivotal time for the global economy. On the
one hand, economic development is characterized by the
"new normal" of higher unemployment, lower productivity
growth, and subdued economic growth that could be derailed
by uncertainties such as geopolitical tensions, the future path
of emerging markets, energy prices, and currency changes.
On the other hand, recent developments show great promise.
The so-called fourth industrial revolution and new ways of
consuming, such as the sharing economy could lead to another
wave of significant innovations that drive growth. Across
countries we are witnessing economic policymaking become
increasingly people-centered and embedded in overall societal
goals (Richard Samans).[1]

---

1   Richard Samans is head of the Center for Global Agenda and member of the
    managing board of the World Economic Forum (see Schwab, 2015, p. xiii).

At the 2016 World Economic Forum (WEF) Klaus Schwab, one of its founders, predicted the advent of a Fourth Industrial Revolution (IR) driven by technology. He emphasized that its unprecedented scale, scope, and complexity would transform the way people live, learn, work, and relate to one another. Schwab did not forecast how this fourth IR would unfold but he stated that solutions need to be integrative, comprehensive, and involve all in society—from academia to industry and both private sectors—to have a positive impact on the global economy and civil society.

Schwab argued that this fourth IR would build on the digital revolution that began last century. Instead of being segmented, as the previous one, it would integrate technologies that void divides between physical, digital, and biological spheres in cyber-physical systems.

Change would develop exponentially, causing major disruptions in management, organizations, education, industry, and government in every country (Schwab, 2016). In positive terms, he highlighted that leaders and organizations able to anticipate and manage disruptions with resilience and agility would find ample opportunities for performance improvement in competitive local and global markets. Conversely, disruptions would be detrimental for complacent organizations reluctant to change and regenerate.

Need for change and global initiatives

The European initiative Europe 2020[2] focuses on strategies to become smart and sustainable, fostering an inclusive economy to meet the challenges of a changing global environment with higher

2   https://ec.europa.eu/info/strategy/european-semester/framework/europe-2020-strategy_en

employment, productivity, and social cohesion. To this end Europe is targeting continuous improvement in five fundamental areas: education, innovation, employment, social inclusion, and climate/energy, all to be reached by 2020.

In 2005 Jeffrey Sachs wrote the book *The End of Poverty: Economic Possibilities for Our Time*. Sachs, an adviser for the United Nations who has worked extensively with mandataries of developed and developing countries in Africa, Asia, and Latin America, went on to predict that extreme poverty would be eradicated by 2015 (Sachs, 2005). In the Preface of his 2015 review of *The End of Poverty* he revised this date to 2030, based on evidence that "the world is not trying hard enough to attain the objective".[3] Sachs, who participated in developing the United Nations 2015 Sustainable Development Goals (SDGs), has stated that these goals will attain the target by 2030.

The 17 SDGs were adopted in September 2015 and represent the UN "world to-do list between 2016 and 2030".[4] The goals are a shared agenda to end poverty, promote peace and opportunities for all, and protect the planet; they are identified in Figure 1.1.

- Goal 1. End poverty in all its forms and everywhere

- Goal 2. End hunger, achieve food security, improved nutrition and promote sustainable agriculture

- Goal 3. Ensure healthy lives and promote wellbeing for all at all ages

- Goal 4. Ensure inclusive quality education for all to promote lifelong learning opportunities for all

---

3   UN Sustainable Development Agenda. Retrieved from http://www.un.org/sustainabledevelopment/development-agenda/

4   UN. 17 Sustainable Development Goals. Retrieved from http://www.un.org/sustainabledevelopment/sustainable-development-goals/

- Goal 5. Achieve gender equality empowering all women and girls
- Goal 6. Ensure availability and sustainable management of water and sanitation for all
- Goal 7. Ensure access to affordable, reliable, sustainable and modern energy for all
- Goal 8. Promote sustained, inclusive and sustainable economic growth, full and productive employment and decent work for all
- Goal 9. Build resilient infrastructure, promote inclusive and sustainable industrialization and foster innovation
- Goal 10. Reduce inequality within and among countries
- Goal 11. Make cities and human settlements inclusive, safe, resilient and sustainable
- Goal 12. Ensure sustainable consumption and production patterns
- Goal 13. Take urgent action to combat climate change and its impacts
- Goal 14. Conserve and sustainably use the oceans, seas and marine resources for sustainable development
- Goal 15. Protect, restore and promote sustainable use of terrestrial ecosystems, sustainably manage forests, combat desertification, and halt and reverse land degradation and halt biodiversity loss
- Goal 16. Promote peaceful and inclusive societies for sustainable development, provide access to justice for all and build effective, accountable and inclusive institutions at all levels

- Goal 17. Strengthen the means of implementation and revitalize the global partnership for sustainable development[5]

FIGURE 1.1   **Sustainable Development Goals**

The Global Infrastructure Initiative

Since 2012, McKinsey & Company's Global Infrastructure Initiative (GII) has convened the world's leaders in infrastructure to identify opportunities to optimize $9 trillion of annual investments. The GII was created as a vehicle to help unlock recurring infrastructure bottlenecks, explore new frontiers, and drive change in the infrastructure industry.

The goal of this initiative is to deliver essential infrastructure quickly and at a lower cost to support economic growth and contribute to building more resilient, stable, and secure communities.

GII has hosted three summits (Istanbul in 2012, Rio de Janeiro in 2014, and San Francisco in 2015) and a series of regional roundtables

5   See more at: http://unfoundationblog.org/common-questions-on-the-global-goals/#sthash.ZAW2edav.dpuf

around the world, laying the foundations for a community of infrastructure leaders committed to pioneering real change. The most recent GII Summit in San Francisco (November 18–20, 2015) explored how innovation and technology can disrupt and improve infrastructure delivery. The fourth GII Summit is scheduled to take place in Singapore in 2017.[6]

People: The DNA of change

It may sound redundant to argue that the human being should be at the center of management and organizations in the 21st century. But despite arguments in favor of positioning people at the center, there is considerable discrepancy between words and deeds; within education, organizations, the economy, and broader society, more attention continues to be paid to other interests beyond the needs and expectations of the people these institutions serve.

Emerging technology created by human talent—the very technology responsible for propelling the speed and extent of global connectivity—is changing the world and affecting the way people live, think, learn, and interact, both socially and in organizations with a significant impact on the economy and society. People have never before had greater opportunities to obtain information so quickly, easily, and cost effectively when making all kinds of decisions.

Around the world at this very moment, human ingenuity is pushing advances in science and technology, fueling innovation, disrupting organizations, propelling economic growth, and reshaping the present and future at an unprecedented speed.

6 McKinsey Global Infrastructure Initiative, http://www.globalinfrastructure initiative.com/

Proper management of data, analytics, semi-conductors, e-commerce, and cyber security are issues that must be effectively managed to optimize potential benefits—and minimize the costs of disruptions—if organizations want to help people.

The **Internet of Things** (IoT) has ignited an unparalleled wave of data analytics, connectivity, and transparency that is radically altering organizations and the way producers and consumers in markets behave and interact across the globe (Turber *et al.*, 2015).[7]

Many say that data analytics will allow us to predict the future along with semi-conductors, which are frequently overlooked as enablers of many ongoing technological developments, fueling innovation with new features, functions, and devices.

Although an exponential amount of information is transmitted over the Internet, security concerns grow and cyberattacks become of critical concern to people and organizations on a global scale.

Companies are preparing for the post-PC world. The exponential growth of mobile devices surpasses any previous form of human communication technology and connectivity. Furthermore, smart and intelligent environments that go beyond space and time enable different human interactions (Follmer, 2015).

---

7   The Internet of Things (IoT) is the network of physical objects—devices, vehicles, buildings, and other items embedded with electronics, software, sensors, and network connectivity that enable all these objects to connect, collect, and exchange data. The IoT allows objects to be controlled remotely across existing network infrastructure; this increased integration of the physical world into computer-based systems can enable improved efficiency, accuracy, and economic benefits. IoT allows technology to encompass cyber-physical systems with smart grids, smart homes, smart cities, intelligent transportation, and personal intelligent phones. Each "thing" is identified through its embedded computing system but is able to interoperate in the Internet Experts estimate that the IoT will consist of almost 50 billion objects by 2020 (according to Wikipedia).

Despite the extensive impact of technology, there is increasing awareness that in the digital age, success comes not from technology itself, but from people, and how people use and interact with technology (Accenture, 2016). Indeed technology may be very useful, but only when people can indeed use it to best effect. The most important technological challenge for the future is how people and organizations can evolve in symbiosis with developments in technology.

Disruptions are the rule today, not the exception, so people, organizations, and the workforce must learn to become agile, updating skills on a constant basis to optimize tech support. According to Accenture (2016), people are the DNA of technology and the engine of change in organizations.

Where people are the DNA of the talent society, sustainable economies, human capital, social corporate responsibility (CSR), national happiness indexes, and inclusive societies, education has a central role; any improvement begins with quality education. In addition to technological skills "Soft Skills" are also needed.

Worldwide, the main gaps in national productivity are rooted in the disconnect between education and the productive sector. Lack of synergy between the supply from education (graduates) and the demands of the labor force (values, attitudes, skills, capacity to solve problems and provide solutions in the workplace) has grown in recent decades because the pace of change and innovation in education lags far behind the speed of change in productive sectors.

This disconnect will persist—increasing the costs of production and unemployment rates—until educational planning is correlated with demands in other sectors. Currently, most analyses are still conducted as if education exists in a vacuum, isolating students from their status as consumers seeking to increase their future productivity and wellbeing.

In addition to the traditional "hard skills" that have been at the core of education since the first industrial revolution, organizations today are increasingly demanding people and graduates with Soft Skills, also termed social, people, and 21st-century skills. Soft Skills are personal abilities and attitudes that enable individuals to get along well with others and are a vital to teams with proven results of increased productivity. Google's Aristotle longitudinal and comprehensive study about the challenges and successes of building the best work teams reviews this in more detail (Duhig, 2016).

Parallel academic research has identified and underlined the need for Soft Skills to improve productivity of the labor force worldwide. Lepeley and Albornoz (2013) found that CEOs of companies that had won the National Quality Award in Chile expressed consensus that education in general—and in business schools in particular—is not developing the Soft Skills that are required in the labor force of the 21st century, including the ability to get along well with other people, communicate effectively, participate in teams, and express empathy. Massaro *et al.* (2016) found similar results in a survey of business schools in Italy, revealing a lack of programs developing Soft Skills to comply with the demands of the labor force. These shortcomings in business schools follow on from failings in middle school. A taskforce study conducted by Tarr and Weeks (2016) on secondary school education in Florida, USA, recommended developing the Soft Skills of students to match the demands of the labor force, thus increasing their chance of finding jobs and thereby decreasing the high unemployment rate among the youth in the millennial generation.

Educate people for the future, not for the past

Larry Page, Google's CEO, has said that people are not being educated to meet the challenges that humankind faces today. He adds that organizations that feel comfortable with what they do are lagging far behind changes in the global environment that are revolutionary, not evolutionary (Gibbs, 2014). Page, who directs one of the fastest growing global tech companies today, highlights that education places too much emphasis on processes and grading instead of serving the needs of students who must confront surmounting challenges as job seekers. He criticizes traditional risk-averse education systems that are hindering the *big thinkers* and discouraging the *risk takers* that Google—and growing numbers of companies worldwide—need to hire.

Here is a summary of his observations:

- Changes that affect humankind are revolutionary, not evolutionary. So incremental changes lead organizations to irrelevance and entropy. Deep transformation is necessary.

- Simplicity of design is the key. Google's search page was one of the simplest sites when it launched in 1997 and still is today.
  - *Simplicity principles* can be applied across all products, services, industries, sectors, and disciplines.

- The internet is one of the most powerful tools in education.
  - Google's Project Loon is a connectivity network that has been providing internet access from high-altitude balloons since 2013 and now entails a network of balloons on the edge of space (flying about twice the altitude of commercial airlines) to provide connectivity worldwide, including across rural and remote areas.

- Education systems are not educating *big thinking*, creative learners, and self-confident, risk-taking graduates, which is creating major obstacles in the productive sector. It is extremely difficult for organizations to shape teams of high achievers when employees have not been educated to be big thinkers and inventors, who are complacent in thinking that it is not possible to innovate, or who are frightened of failure.

The above concerns are evident in Google's hiring strategies. Recruiters invest more time and effort in personal interviews with prospective employees to recruit big thinkers and entrepreneurial-type risk-takers with strong Soft Skills, essential to build effective teams, over considerations of school grades, academic degrees, and other accolades.

Google's hiring practices are rapidly spreading to other organizations, industries, and across sectors and international borders. Moreover, this new recruiting strategy is inducing progressive business schools and universities to select prospective students based on the potential for future achievement promised by their Soft Skills, rather than relying on past grade performance.

This is the academic reaction, at least in part, to recurrent arguments that many technology talents and 21st century gurus, who are among the wealthiest people in the world, have been college dropouts. Among them are Bill Gates and co-founder Paul Allen of Microsoft, Mark Zuckerberg of Facebook, Larry Ellison of Oracle, Steve Jobs of Apple, Michael Dell of Dell Inc., Elon Musk of PayPal, Evan Williams and Jack Dorsey of Twitter, Arash Ferdowsi of DropBox, Daniel Ek of Spotify, Evan Spiegel of Snapchat, Alexa von Tobel of LearnVest, and Sean Parker and Shawn Fanning of Napster (*The Guardian*, 2014).

Nonetheless, this link by no means diminishes the value of education. On the contrary, it shows the important of education, and the responsibility we have to provide the right kind of education, based on the significant impact it has on the productivity of organizations that drive the economy and society.

These same concerns apply to the need for effective integration between different levels of education. Most of the constraints to assessing future success based on past school performance (to advance from nursery to kindergarten, elementary to secondary, high school to college, or from education to organizations in the labor force) are embedded in ineffective articulation between educational systems and organizations that shape markets and the economy. Such poor communication is most likely to occur within society when education displaces the human being from the center of attention.

Education and development: Problem or opportunity?

The massive and unstoppable growth of information propelled by technology, the internet, and global connectivity is disrupting people and organizations in all productive sectors, governments, economies, and societies worldwide, inflicting significant changes in the development and delivery of education programs at all levels.

The impact of education on economic growth and social development is important, but measuring impact isolated from other factors is complex and elusive. This is the main obstacle for effective dialogue between education and organizations in the labor force and is why the subject escapes the attention it needs. Fortunately things are changing, influenced by shifts in demand for skills in the labor force which are underlined by stubbornly high and indeed increasing rates of unemployment in some sectors and demographics, and the shortage of skilled labor to meet demands in many sectors.

Global growth

The main components of global growth that drive economic expansion—or contraction—are consumption and investment. This is no different to an individual managing personal finances, spending more on purchases when personal income increases and investing a larger proportion for retirement when there is more money to spare. The same pattern occurs within countries and the global economy. Table 1.1 shows that between 2005 and 2014 global wealth grew at an average of 2.47% per year, led largely by consumption (including government consumption which on average is about one-sixth of private consumption) and investment. In the last decade the world benefited from economic growth in nine out of ten years.

TABLE 1.1   Global growth 2005–2014

Year	Growth rate (%)
2005	3.6
2006	4.1
2007	3.8
2008	1.4
2009	−2.1
2010	4.1
2011	2.8
2012	2.2
2013	2.3
2014	2.5

Source: Economic Intelligence Unit (EIU), November 2015. In 2015 Report of the International Labor Organization (p.15)

Global wealth and global workforce

The global economy experienced very slow recovery in output levels after the last contraction, and employment creation by 2016 was still insufficient to close the global employment gap. Employment gaps are due to decreases in available employment, yet commonly omit lower labor force participation, which can occur when large proportions of job seekers drop out of employment when hiring is significantly lower during peak unemployment periods. Global employment grew at an average annual rate of 1.7% between 1991 and 2007, and slowed to 1.2% between 2007 and 2014 (ILO, 2015, p. 16).

It is expected that job creation will remain low over the medium term, thus widening the global employment gap. Furthermore, with graduates trying to enter the labor market, estimates indicate that 280 million jobs will need to be created over the coming five years to close the global employment gap (*ibid.*).

Global unemployment increased between 2013 and 2014, when an average 5.9% of the world labor force was without a job. However, there are wide variations across regions and countries. North Africa, sub-Saharan Africa, and the Middle East continue to experience high rates of unemployment, in some cases as high as 30% of the national labor force. Southern European countries do not show significant declines in unemployment rates. Asian countries—particularly in South-East Asia and the Pacific—are experiencing lower rates of unemployment, but often with high levels of informal employment which in some countries reaches 85% of total employment (*ibid.*).

Among developed economies, while unemployment fell significantly in the United Kingdom and the United States, other countries in the European Union show smaller decreases. In Latin America and the Caribbean, several countries faced growing unemployment because of a slowing global economy that reversed previously high rates of job creation (*ibid.*).

A significant concern among economists is that long-term unemployment trends may indicate further declines, with participation rates predicted to fall below 63% of the global working-age population by 2030 (*ibid.*). Such decreases in labor force participation not only lower growth potential in affected economies, but may reflect changing demographics and the discouragement effects of persistence crisis; each presents significant challenges to decreasing the world income inequality gap.

Youth unemployment is a global problem: Implications for education

In developed economies and the EU, falling work participation rates among millennials (18–34 years old) are related to persistently weak job prospects. Some trends may reverse, with faster economic growth in the medium term. In emerging economies, especially in South Asia, participation rates have fallen among graduates and women; these trends are likely to be long term (ILO, 2015, p. 19).

Younger people in the 15–24 years bracket continue to show disproportionately high rates of unemployment. The global youth unemployment rate reached 13% in 2014, almost three times higher than the unemployment rate for adults. Although new youth cohorts entering the labor market are smaller than previous generations because of lower birth rates in East Asia and Latin America, it remains difficult for young people in most countries to find jobs.

The most puzzling concern for 21st-century education is that unemployment trends persist in spite of considerable improvements in average graduation rates within these youth cohorts. Although the share of youths with tertiary education participating in the labor force has increased since 2007 in 26 out of 30 countries, unemployment rates among young workers with tertiary education have risen in 16 out of 18 countries and many countries are projecting substantial increases in youth unemployment (ILO, 2015). This evidence confirms Page's concerns that education is not training students to meet labor force demands (Gibbs, 2014).

The ILO predicted that the global youth unemployment rate would increase to over 13% in 2015, and remain unchanged until 2018. The largest increases in 2015 would be in East Asia and the Middle East, with further expected increases over the following years. This concerning global picture presents significant challenges to education systems across the world, which face growing levels of frustration among graduates unable to find jobs and, in many cases, confronting repayment of student loans. The generation of millennials contrasts deeply with employment trends among older persons who tend to fare better than their younger counterparts (ILO, 2015, p. 21).

Labor markets

Older workers

Unlike previous economic downturns, when older workers were pushed into early retirement, this time enterprises around the world have held on to their most experienced workers. However, for older workers who do lose their jobs, it is increasingly difficult to obtain new employment.

Women

The gender gap in the labor market persists. Although the last economic contraction resulted in a moderate decrease, as job losses were concentrated in male-dominated industries, recovery in employment occurred mostly in sectors employing predominantly men (e.g. construction), thus reopening the gender gap (*ibid.*).

Overall, women continue to experience higher rates of unemployment and are less likely than men to participate in the labor force when unemployment rates are high. But over the last four decades, a consistent trend indicates that more women are opting to undertake entrepreneurial activity as a source of income, because it better matches women's need for flexible work, accommodating multiple roles and responsibilities (workers, parenting, caregivers) (Guerra *et al.*, 2016; Kuschel and Lepeley, 2016; Lepeley *et al.*, 2015).

While in the short run, entrepreneurship endeavors at the start-up phase have higher risks than other sources of employment, in the long term this business opportunity provides an important source of employment for increasing numbers of women worldwide, and a particularly lucrative way to secure income in countries with well-established market economies (Lepeley *et al.*, 2015).

Women's participation in entrepreneurial activity due to *necessity* is more common in lower income countries in Africa, where women need an activity that provides income in order to maintain a family. Entrepreneurship propelled by *opportunity* expands faster in market economies than in more centralized systems.

Opportunity entrepreneurship and start-ups among women has increased in direct proportion with the number of women completing tertiary education in STEM (science, technology, and engineering) across the world. Studies conducted by Kuschel and Lepeley (2015) report that the number of start-ups led by women has developed due to increases in women's higher educational attainment and is also based on joint ventures with male university classmates who become partners in business and partners in life (Kuschel and

Lepeley, 2016). Findings of this research show that business part-nerships may continue after workmates divorce.

This gender gap is of great concern because women are the majority (52%) of the global population, meaning that gaps in women's compensation accrue to substantial loss in overall income, and hinder economic development. In countries and regions with large income gaps, losses can reach up to 30% of GDP per capita. The gender gap must be addressed as a central development con-cern if sustainable economies and inclusive societies are to be achieved worldwide (Lepeley *et al.*, 2015).

Job creation prospects

The ILO predicts that job creation in the near future will be mainly through expansion in the service sector. The bulk of new jobs will be created in the private sector while public services in health care, education, and administration will show smaller increases.

Global industrial employment is expected to stabilize, driven by rising employment in construction. But the sector will contribute little to recovery of employment rates, despite its important role in structural transformation, particularly so in emerging economies (ILO, 2015, p. 23).

Manufacturing industries will continue to lose jobs. Although developed countries account for the largest share of manufacturing jobs, some developing countries are experiencing falls in manufac-turing employment, in spite of the fact that manufacturing indus-tries have not reached levels comparable to developed nations.

The service sector is expected to be the most dynamic area of job creation worldwide in the next decade (*ibid.*).

Human talent and growing demand for high skills

Low-skilled occupations and manual jobs make up about 45% of total employment worldwide. Medium-skilled jobs account for 37%. In comparison, the demand for high-skilled jobs comprises 18% of total employment and it is increasing steadily. These trends will continue with significant regional variations.

Medium-skilled jobs are declining in developed countries, partly replaced by low-skilled occupations, but remain stable as a share of the global economy. The share of high-skilled occupations varies widely, ranging from less than 10% in sub-Saharan Africa to close to 40% in developed economies (*ibid.*).

Job market shifts and increased inequality

In the "knowledge society" of the 21st century, the decline of medium-skilled jobs in developed nations is one of the most important factors contributing to rising inequality and the so-called "hollowing-out" of middle income jobs (*ibid.*).

Job market projections are instrumental for education because, to a great extent, economic growth and social development in developed and developing countries alike will depend on congruency and synchronization between outcomes of educational systems and labor market demands.

Will education be able to fulfill its responsibility to meet the forthcoming demands of labor markets? Is alignment between all educational levels adequate to comply with the social responsibility that educators and education have within society?

In the same fashion that corporate social responsibility is today a critical issue in ethical business practice and increasingly in government-affiliated entities, education, whether from private or public providers, must fulfill a role of social responsibility with regard to organizations and broader society (Goleman, 2006).

2

Human-Centered Management (HCM): Roots and evolution

The human-centered imperative is not new. Albeit under other names, it has been a recurrent concern of organization scholars for over a century, a reaction to the machine- and process-focused administrative structures of the industrial past.

The Human-Centered Management model for Quality and Sustainability (HCMxSQ) presented in this book is built on the sources discussed in this chapter. These foundations helped to articulate a multidisciplinary analytical framework coherent with the needs of people and organizations of the 21st century that are confronting constant disruptions, yet seeking continuous improvement to achieve organization sustainability (Hanauer and Beinhocker, 2014).

This is the era of knowledge, information, and global connectivity; in spite of its undeniable benefits, this has created uncertain and volatile organizational environments where human capital, talent management, resilience, agility, and quality standards become keys for innovation and sustainability.

Under these conditions, the success of Human-Centered Management depends on effective synchronization of customers' needs with the demands of the external environment and with strategies that satisfy the needs of the people who work within and for organizations.[1] Organizations unable to meet the needs of customers in sync with the needs of the people who produce its products and services will be increasingly unfit to become sustainable in the 21st century.

Human emotions and economic actions have been linked throughout economic history. The British visionary Adam Smith (1723–1790), father of modern economics, wrote *The Theory of Moral Sentiments*—pioneering the importance of people and their behavior in organizations and society—in 1759, almost 20 years before he wrote his economic masterpiece, *The Wealth of Nations*.

Joseph Schumpeter (1883–1950) was an Austrian-born American economist who became a Harvard professor in 1932. He is considered one of the most influential economists of the 20th century, popularizing the economic concept **creative destruction**. It refers to the talent of people and entrepreneurs who subdue obsolete structures, replacing them with new ones that change the economy and build a better society (Schumpeter, 1936, 1939, 1950).

At this point it is useful to recall two recognized organizational developments of the industrial age. Not because they positioned humans at the center, but because at the beginning of the 20th century both models contributed to bring order to organizations that until

---

1   The concepts *in* and *for* explicitly recognize that people not only work *in* the physical facilities of an organization but also work *for* the organization in fulfillment of a personal commitment to advance the mission, vision, values, and goals of the organization.

then were disorganized and lacked rational and scientific approaches. Organizations became better organized after Max Weber in Germany and Frederick Taylor in the United States paralleled new developments in administration theories (Woodward, 1965).

Max Weber (1864–1920), a sociologist and political economist, developed the concept of the normative bureaucratic organization on top of a rigid hierarchical structure of rules and commands that exists to this day (Weber, 1920). Frederick Winslow Taylor (1856–1915), a mechanical engineer who sought to improve efficiency in the industrial society, pioneered the efficiency movement in organizations and became the founder of modern management. The Academy of Management's publication of the most influential management books of the 20th century ranks Taylor's book *The Principles of Scientific Management* (1911) as one of the most influential.[2] The book is based on Taylor's fundamental philosophy of using the rule of knowledge to develop organizations.

Strong criticism of the bureaucratic organization was led by Ludwig von Mises, another European and professor of the Austrian School of Economics. In his 1944 book *Bureaucracy*, he examined the nature of people's control in bureaucracies and contrasted this with market systems that protect people's freedom to choose. Von Mises argued that in market system, entrepreneurs serve the needs of consumers and are driven by the interest to earn a living by making profits and avoiding losses. Comparatively, bureaucracies—particularly government agencies and bureaus—are ruled by strict regulations and prescriptive laws that coerce employees to comply with commands of superiors. Von Mises argues that these

---

2   The most influential management books of the 20th century were chosen by 137 senior members of the Academy of Management in 2001 (Bedeian and Wren, 2001).

hierarchies, operating under rigid norms, curtail public service and the satisfaction of users' needs (Von Mises, 1949).

In 1974, the Austrian Friedrich Hayek and Swede Gunnar Myrdal received the Nobel Prize in Economic Sciences for their studies in how people benefited from the integration of organizations, the economy, and society.

In 1979, the American economist Theodore Schultz was granted the Nobel Prize for pioneering theories regarding investment in people and education to improve economic development and society. In 1992 another American economist, Gary Becker, won the Nobel Prize in Economic Sciences for his work on human capital theories, which demonstrated considerable convergence with Schultz's. Both were professors of the University of Chicago.

The foundations of Human-Centered Management

Elton Mayo: Hawthorne Studies

In management science the human focus as a critical organization driver started in 1933 with the book *The Human Problems of an Industrial Civilization* by Elton Mayo.[3] His book, also among the most influential management books of the 20th century, was based on data Mayo collected in the famous Hawthorne Studies (1924–1932) at the Western Electric company near Chicago.

The **Hawthorne effect** *(The Economist, 2008)* study pioneered productivity assessment in the labor force, correlating improvements

---

3   Elton Mayo was an Australian-born US sociologist and professor of industrial research at Harvard who studied the effects of emotional factors on employees' behavior, identifying powerful relationships between personal satisfaction and productivity in the workplace.

in the working environment with employees' satisfaction in the workplace. Results showed that performance improved when managers showed care for the working environment of a group of employees in a factory compared with a control group without intervention. When the study ended and the intervention stopped, employees' productivity plummeted. The Hawthorne effect also showed that employees are more responsive to group involvement and social satisfaction than to financial incentives. The study pioneered the theory that productivity increases when managers care for people and started a trend that employees place greater value on managers' concern for their wellbeing than on monetary rewards.

Maslow: Hierarchy of human needs

> Human life will never be understood unless higher aspirations are taken into account. Growth, self-actualization, striving for health, quest for identity and autonomy, yearning for excellence must be accepted beyond question as a widespread and perhaps universal human tendency (Maslow, 1954, pp. xii-xiii).

Abraham Maslow's Hierarchy of Human Needs introduced in his 1943 paper "A theory of human motivation" revolutionized the emerging discipline of management. His book *Motivation and Personality* (1954) is also in the Academy of Management list of the most influential of the 20th century and his hierarchy of needs remains a "classic among classics" (Bedeian and Wren, 2001).

In contrast with mainstream psychologists such as Freud and Skinner, who focused on pathological behavior, depression, and the underpinnings of human unhappiness, Maslow pioneered studies on behavior of normal and thriving people, who for practical purposes, are the majority (Maslow, 1999; Seligman, 2004; Uchida and Oichi, 2016). Maslow's attention to happy individuals and their psychological trajectory broke away from old standards. This new perspective led him to define the hierarchy of human needs that every person has to fulfill to reach higher motivations.

Figure 2.1 shows the sequence of the hierarchy of human needs, adapted by this author. Like Maslow's scale, this advances from basic needs (food, shelter, security), to a second level (love, affection, respect), to the third level (economic needs), fourth level (self-actualization, intellectual needs), and finally a fifth level (altruistic and spiritual needs). In this case Maslow's hierarchical pyramid has been replaced by circles of overlapping relationships to show the cycle of needs building up to generate higher needs, as Maslow expressed it.

FIGURE 2.1   **Hierarchy of human needs**

Source: Author's adaptation of Maslow's hierarchy of needs

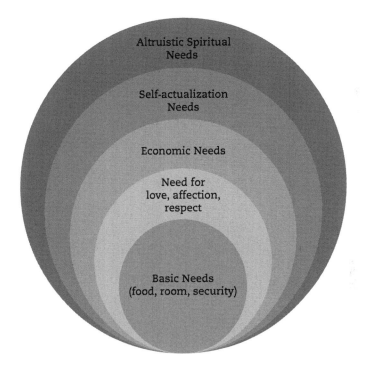

Maslow pioneered the search for happiness, emphasizing it as a critical human state that required more attention and further study. Despite this, it took half a century of cross-fertilization between psychology and economics to introduce the happiness construct to economics and management (Frey and Stutzer, 2010).

One of Maslow's most compelling findings is that the need for self-actualization and learning is always present in the human psyche, but it surges after basic needs have been satisfied. This finding has important implications for organizations, performance, and productivity, which until now have been underestimated.

In the last decade, research on happiness has proliferated and today a growing number of countries are joining the ranks of the National Happiness Report and Wellbeing Index, capturing the attention of scholars and governments worldwide (Helliwell *et al.*, 2015; Coy, 2015).

Douglas McGregor: The human side of the enterprise

Douglas McGregor was a mechanical engineer who obtained a PhD in psychology from Harvard University. He was professor at MIT Sloan School of Management and author of the book *The Human Side of Enterprise* (1960), also listed among the 25 most influential management books of the 20th century. In this book he developed Theory X and Theory Y, where he contrasts managers' assumptions and behaviors that determine how organizations deal with employees under bureaucratic structures and matrix organizations.

Table 2.1 shows McGregor's comparison of the fundamental principles of Theory X and Theory Y.

TABLE 2.1   Theory X and Theory Y

Theory "X" (industrial era)	Theory "Y" (Human-Centered Management)
People do not like to work	People like to work when they are satisfied
Most people think work is an inconvenience	People like to assume responsibilities
People only work to earn income to live	Most people feel proud of their work
It is necessary to force people to do their jobs	Most people feel glad to work in a suitable environment
People avoid responsibilities	People value to be trusted and feel responsible
It is necessary to control people constantly to perform their work	It is necessary to provide clear guidelines and freedom for people to perform effectively at work
The most effective method to induce people to work is to increase their sense of job security and then threaten them with job losses	People are encouraged to fulfill the mission of the organization when they are satisfied with the organizational climate, work in teams, have access to effective information flow, and receive AFFECTIVE[4] and effective support from leaders and supervisors.

Although the characteristics of Theory X may appear radical and excessive, they are still common practice in organizations and regions around the world.

The *Organizational Psychology and Organizational Behavior Journal* produced a video on Group Affect that dwells on a comprehensive disclosure of the meaning and uses of *Affection* (Barsade and Knight, 2015).[5] Increasing numbers of organization development researchers are emphasizing the importance of Soft Skills, the use of empathy, and respect for others, given the powerful positive effects on employees' self-confidence that have been demonstrated (Basford and

---

4   Group Affect. YouTube video presentation recorded January 5, 2016. Retrieved from https://www.youtube.com/watch?v=CmVlaEz6UoQ

5   *Ibid.*

Schaninger, 2016). A recent broad range study conducted by Google as part of Project Aristotle on Perfect Teams, found that members of the most effective teams have special characteristics of rapport, empathy, and respect associated with Theory Y (Duhig, 2016).

Geert Hofstede: Organization cultures and global implications

Geert Hofstede is a Dutch social psychologist and Professor Emeritus of Organizational Anthropology and International Management at Maastricht University in the Netherlands. He has also worked at IBM where he conducted extensive studies, pioneering research on cross-cultural groups and organizations that led to the development of his cultural dimensions theory published in his book *Cultures and Organizations: The Software of the Mind* (2010). Hofstede identifies a six-dimension framework that facilitates understanding of people's behavior in organizations with valuable implications for leadership and management.

Hofstede's detailed definitions of the Six Dimensions are as follows:

- **Power distance index (PDI)**. Measures the degree of power that members of an organization or society accept. Groups that exhibit a high degree of power distance accept hierarchies and receive orders without much justification. Organizations and societies with low power distance tend to equalize power, strive for equality, and demand justification for inequality.

- **Individualism versus collectivism (IDV)**. Individualism is characterized by preference for a loosely knit social framework where people tend to care for their own wellbeing over the wellbeing of the group. Collectivism is associated with close-knit groups, organizations, or societies. In practical terms, this refers to whether people's self-image is defined in terms of "I" or "we".

- **Masculinity versus femininity (MAS).** The masculinity dimension is associated with achievement, assertiveness, competitiveness, and material reward for success. The femininity dimension shows preference for cooperation, modesty, empathy, and consensus-orientation. Hofstede sees that in the organizational context, masculinity versus femininity relates to "tough versus tender" cultures.

- **Uncertainty avoidance index (UAI).** This measures the degree of tolerance and resilience of people for uncertainty and ambiguity. The fundamental issue here is how a group, organization, and society can deal with a highly uncertain future versus high control over the future. Teams, organizations, or countries that exhibit high levels of UAI tend to maintain rigid codes of belief and behavior and are intolerant of unorthodox behavior and ideas. Low or weak UAI groups accept a relaxed attitude where practice counts more than principles.

- **Long-term orientation versus short-term normative orientation (LTO).** All groups, organizations, and societies retain some traditions of the past while dealing with the challenges of the present and the future. Teams prioritize these two existential goals differently. Groups that show short-term orientation opt to keep time-honored traditions and norms, viewing change with suspicion. Groups with long-term orientation are more pragmatic about encouraging change and make efforts to prepare for the future.

- **Indulgence versus restraint (IND)**. Indulgence prevails in groups that follow relatively freer gratification of basic and natural human drives associated with enjoying life and having fun. Restraint prevails in groups and societies that suppress gratification of needs and have strict social norms.

Table 2.2 contrasts patterns associated with industrial organization structures (Characteristics 1) and Human-Centered Management (Characteristics 2) (Hofstede et al., 2010).

TABLE 2.2 **Hofstede's six-dimension framework**

Dimension	Characteristics 1	Characteristics 2
Power distance	High: Acceptance of hierarchical order	Low: Equalize power distribution
Uncertainty avoidance	High: uncomfortable with uncertainty and ambiguity	Low: comfortable with uncertainty and ambiguity
Individualism versus collectivism	Prevalence of individual interests	Prevalence of collective interests
Masculinity vs. femininity	Male: tough, achievement, assertiveness material rewards, success, competitiveness	Female: tender, cooperative, modesty, caring for others, life quality, consensus-oriented
Orientation	Long-term orientation	Short-term orientation
Indulgence vs. restraint	Indulgence and gratification of human drives, joy and fun	Restraint, suppresses gratification of needs, follows strict social norms

Identifying individual preferences and group dynamics as per Hofstede's model help leaders and organizations optimize efforts to change and improve the organizational climate (Bains, 2015).

Change, risk, and resilience

Psychologically, economic change is challenging for people, teams, and organizations largely because the costs derived from change are unpredictable and the benefits are intangible. Change involves risk; the level of risk depends on the willingness of people and leaders to assume responsibility for change. But in the 21st century change is not an option, it is an imperative. Organizations anchored in hierarchical and bureaucratic structures of the industrial past will pay the price of postponing efforts to become competitive in increasingly transparent evolving markets.

Every organization is different and in order to advance it is necessary to conduct constant reassessment of the present in comparison with an imagined—more desirable— future, and assess the costs and benefits of disruptions.

Management innovation

Peter Drucker: The knowledge worker

In 1954 Peter Drucker, an Austrian-born American, educator, and management consultant wrote the book *The Practice of Management*.[6] This book is ranked the third most important management book of the 20th century, granting Drucker recognition as the founder of management education (Bedeian and Wren, 2001). Drucker explored how people are organized in businesses, government, and non-profit organizations. He was a visionary who predicted major developments that would affect management in later years including, among others, increasing privatization and decentralization, and the emergence of an information society that would embed lifelong learning

6   The Peter Drucker Institute, http://www.druckerinstitute.com/

as a necessity (Drucker, 1964). In his book *Landmarks of Tomorrow* (Drucker, 1959) he forecasted a rapid expansion of the knowledge society and the emergence of the "Knowledge Workers" whose productivity would reach the next management frontier (Kardos, 2012).

Chris Argyris: The learning organization

Chris Argyris, an American professor of Harvard who studied psychology, physiology, and organizational behavior, became known by his seminal work *Learning Organizations*.[7] In his book *Personality and Organization: The Conflict between the System and the Individual*, also listed among the most influential management books of the 20th century (Bedeian and Wren, 2001), Argyris explored the effects of organizational structure on individuals, and how managers can adopt management patterns that integrate the needs of individual workers with the demands of the organization (Argyris, 1957). In his books *Interpersonal Competence and Organizational Effectiveness* (1962) and *Organization and Innovation* (1965), he focused on organizational change and the behavior of senior executives.

Edwards Deming: The father of total quality management

Edwards Deming is the father of Total Quality Management (TQM). His book *Quality, Productivity and Competitive Position* (Deming, 1982b), also among the most influential management books of the 20th century, is comparable in creative stature to the previous scholars but differs in an important aspect. Until this point, management and organization scholars had analyzed internal issues in organizations, such as human relations, productivity, leadership, structure, and strategies, while economists made separate analyses of external

---

7   http://thinkers50.com/blog/chris-argyris-1923-2013-appreciation/

organizational challenges such as customers, markets, and demands. Deming argued that integrating an organization's external with its internal challenges is a necessary condition to attain continuous improvement, demonstrate quality standards, and secure an organization's sustainability (Deming, 1994).

TQM is based on equating the satisfaction of external customers—who buy or receive products or services from an organization—with the wellbeing of the people who work in the organization, and need to continuously improve their productivity to create products and services that meet the approval of consumers. Nobody can give to others something they do not have. Consequently if employees are not satisfied with working conditions in the organization, the challenges to achieve continuous improvement are insurmountable, the costs of production and time waste are higher, and organization competitiveness lower.

Deming was an American engineer, statistician, professor, author, lecturer, and management consultant, who started his career as an electrical engineer. He specialized in mathematical physics and participated in the development of sampling methods used by the U.S. Department of the Census and the Bureau of Labor Statistics. He later worked in Japan where he found fertile industrial and cultural ground to develop the TQM model in cooperation with Japanese scholars. Deming's customer-focused management strategies are often credited as the driving force behind Toyota's surge as one of the most prolific car manufacturers of last century as well as the capacity of post-war Japan to become the second most powerful economy in the world in just one decade.[8]

---

8   Toyota is often cited as an example of a customer-focused automobile manufacturer corporation that in less than a decade invaded the roads of the world with smaller Japanese cars that met the needs of consumers unable to afford large American cars at the height of the petroleum crisis.

Deming worked in Japan and other countries while he was developing his TQM model, gaining extensive international experience to provide the validity and reliability necessary to consolidate TQM as a global transformation force.

In the late 1980s, the human-centered principles and practices of Deming's TQM became so influential that they were adopted as the framework to create National Quality Award programs (NQAs) around the world. In retrospect, NQAs have helped thousands of corporations and organizations around the world to deploy efficiency innovations, putting people first.[9]

Efficiency innovation is today a constant pursuit in business and organizations, and is seen as a determinant factor in attaining sustainability. The effectiveness of efficiency innovation grows in direct proportion to the volume of information available to people, how effectively and efficiently people manage information, and the transparency of markets.

Organizations of all kinds need to continuously increase productivity in order to achieve competitive advantages, gain customers, clients or users, and remain in business. Therefore continuous performance assessment is a constant concern for businesses and organizations, overall because the days of controlled and privileged usage of information are on the way to extinction, as are the monopolies and oligopolistic power that in the past allowed producers to control quantities and prices, to the detriment of clients.

The power to control information was gone when the information revolution began. Today concentration of power that creates monopolies and oligopolies is increasingly rare as customers gain

---

9   NQAs started to help the productive sector (manufacture industries, corporate business, large and small) and later were created in the service sector (education and health) when it was realized that the capacity of the workforce was directly related with wellbeing of people where education and health care have a significant impact.

access to open sources of information available on the internet and social networks.

In his book *Out of the Crisis* Deming (1982a) summarizes principles and practices of his quality management construct which are summarized in "14 Points for Management" below:

1. Empower people with commitment to continuous improvement of product and service aiming to become competitive, create sustainable business, and generate new jobs.

2. Adopt the new philosophy. We are in a new economic age. Management must awaken to the challenge, learn their responsibilities and take on leadership for change.

3. Eliminate need for inspection on a mass basis. Start building quality into products from the very beginning.

4. End practice of rewarding business based on price tags. Instead, minimize total cost by moving toward long-term relationships with customers based on loyalty and trust.

5. Improve constantly the system of production and service to reach quality standards leading to increased productivity and decreasing costs.

6. Institute continuous improvement on the job training because knowledge changes constantly and at a fast pace.

7. Supervision of senior management is in need of an overhaul. Responsible leadership is necessary to help people do a better job.

8. Drive out fear, so everyone can get work *in* the organization and have their needs satisfied to work *for* the organization as well.

9. Break down barriers between departments so people can work in teams and develop a collective vison to anticipate problems in production before product failures.

10. Eliminate exhortations of zero defects in the workplace. Such slogans create adversarial relationships among people and underscore evidence that most product failures and low productivity are rooted in the system and beyond the power of employees.

11. Eliminate management by objective and numbers and substitute by effective participatory leadership.

12. Remove barriers that rob employees of their right to be proud of their work. The responsibility of supervisors must be changed from quantity and crude numbers attainment to continuous improvement leading to quality standards.

13. Institute a vigorous program of education and self-improvement for everybody in the organization.

14. Put everybody in the company to work to accomplish the transformation. Organizational transformation is everybody's job and responsibility.

National Quality Award (NQA) programs around the world

In 1951 Japan was the first country to create the Deming National Quality Award sponsored by the Japanese Union of Scientists and Engineers.[10] In 1987 the United States established the Malcolm Baldrige National Quality Award Program to foster productivity and competitiveness in manufacturing, business, and corporations of

10 https://www.juse.or.jp/deming_en/award/

all sizes.[11] In 2001 the Baldrige Award was expanded to recognize service organizations that deployed the Baldrige Model in education[12] and health care[13] sectors and again in 2007 to include non-profit and government organization awards.[14]

The Baldrige Award is now known as the Baldrige Performance Excellence Program. The name change was driven by widespread use of the term "quality" as a qualifying adjective unrelated to continuous improvement standards that degraded the true value of the quality concept. This forced National Quality Awards around the world to substitute the quality term by performance excellence, to highlight the continuous improvement imperative of rigorous global standards of quality.

The European Quality Award was created in 1991, sponsored by the European Foundation of Quality Management (EFQM).[15] Although it kept the Q for quality in the acronym EFQM, it changed the name of the program to EFQM Excellence Program.

Numerous countries in Latin America established National Quality Award programs in the 1990s, including Brazil, Chile, Colombia, Ecuador, and Peru.[16]

11   https://www.nist.gov/baldrige
12   http://www.nist.gov/baldrige/enter/education.cfm
13   http://www.nist.gov/baldrige/enter/health_care.cfm
14   http://www.nist.gov/baldrige/enter/nonprofit.cfm. The author was a member of the Baldrige Board of Examiners between 2002 and 2005. She initiated a petition to create a Baldrige NQA for non-profit and government organizations, which was implemented in 2007.
15   European Foundation of Quality Management (EFQM). http://www.efqm. org/what-we-do/recognition/efqm-excellence-award
16   National Quality Foundation (FNQ), Brazil, http://www.fnq.org.br/english; ChileCalidad, http://www.chilecalidad.cl/; Premio Nacional a la Calidad Corporacion Calidad Colombia, https://corporacioncalidad.org/; Corporación Ecuatoriana de la Calidad Total, Ecuador, http://www.calidadtotal. org/; Premio Nacional a la Calidad del Perú, http://www.cdi.org.pe/premio_ presentacion.htm

I served for five years on the Board of Examiners of the Baldrige National Quality Award Program and I have been adviser to the National Quality Award programs in the aforementioned countries. My duty to evaluate applicants' performance and observe the significant improvements they reached in customer service satisfaction and revenues as the result of enhanced work environment, employee wellbeing, social corporate responsibility, and significant increases in productivity, were the most important motivation to adopt Baldrige principles and practices and adapt them to develop an ad hoc model, write books on quality management, and lecture on the subject in countries worldwide. It became vital for me to show urbi et orbi the benefits that the deployment of a systematic quality achievement methodology has for people and organizations. Moreover, it was critical to convey how the pursuit of continuous improvement, which is helping an elite of organizations affiliated with quality and excellence awards worldwide, has to become accessible to organizations pursuing quality standards in all industries and sectors which today is a requirement to attain sustainability in the increasingly competitive global economy.

In 2001 I wrote the book *Management and Quality in Education: A Model for Assessment*, where I adopted Baldrige principles and adapted them to provide a methodology for improving education as a fundamental element of organizational improvement and economic development.

3

Disruptions: Challenges or opportunities?

Chapter 2 presented a historical perspective on organization development and the theoretical evolution leading to the human-centered paradigm shift that originated as a reaction to hierarchical, bureaucratic, machine-oriented theories of administration of Weber and of Taylor that predominated during the Industrial Revolution. It considered the people-oriented organization anchored in the theories of Mayo, Maslow, and McGregor, and the genesis of management with Drucker and Deming, that prevail today.

Now it is time to look at the future of management. In this context I will discuss the main disruptions that selected primary sources from across the world identify as the main changes that will affect management.

Awareness of disruptions is critical in management because their impacts will affect all organizations, economies, and societies worldwide, and these will be deep and far reaching.

The effects of disruptions are exacerbated by the speed of change and by a level of global connectivity with no precedent in human history. Consequences are difficult to predict, but one thing is for sure: disruptions have a double effect potential. On one hand disruptions can present opportunities for change and considerable benefits for people, organizations, and societies prepared to deal with the accompanying challenges. On the other hand, disruptions will be harmful when people and organizations are unprepared to face unavoidable challenges.

This chapter discusses disruptions from a global perspective to raise awareness of the importance of early preparation for dealing with the unavoidable.

The beginning of this book cited the concerns of Klaus Schwab, one of the founders of the World Economic Forum, who was explicit about the consequences of a Fourth Industrial Revolution; namely, he believes it will bring about deep disruptions that will transform the way people live, learn, work, and relate to one another. He highlighted that the scale, scope, and complexity of the transformation will be driven by technology, and it will be unlike anything humankind has experienced affecting all sectors, industries, and organizations.

The following discussion presents a series of disruptions that are affecting management and organizations today with potential to peak in the near future, across the world.

The list is not exhaustive but serves as a guide to facilitate identification of major disruptions that organizations will confront, and presses for increasing capacity to forecast the future and foresee integrative solutions, locally and globally.

Global disruptions

Dobbs *et al.* (2015) in the book *No Ordinary Disruption* identify four global forces that will break historic trends in the coming future. In agreement with Schwab, Dobbs *et al.* (2015) identify technology as one of the major disruptive forces. They add urbanization, migration of people and aging populations as major global disruptions in the near future.

Urbanization

A trend disrupting nations around the world—and particularly developing countries—is urbanization. Although people have been moving to cities for centuries, the scale and pace of today's urbanization has no precedent. Urbanization is driven by higher incomes and opportunities for a better life, but also the opportunity to leave behind deteriorating rural living conditions and low returns on small-scale agriculture.

The world is in the midst of one of the largest mass migrations from the countryside to the city. While Europe and the United States began processes of urbanization in the 18th and 19th centuries, in the 21st century Latin America, China, and India (each with a population of more than a billion people) have begun show large urban shifts (Dobbs *et al.*, 2015).

In 2014, 54% of people across the globe were living in cities. The number is expected to double (to approximately 6.4 billion) by 2050, turning much of the world into a global city (IOM, 2015).

Although migrations and human mobility play critical roles in generating economic sustainability and inclusive societies, city management and governments around the world still do not give migration the attention that it requires, given associated disruption of urban development planning, and significant effects on education, organizations, the economic system and levels of inclusiveness in society (Dobbs *et al.*, 2015).

Jonathan Woetzel (2016), director of the McKinsey Global Institute, in his presentation *Inclusive Cities are Productive Cities,* said that when we look at major cities, most are indeed immigrant hubs, including New York, London, Los Angeles, Shanghai, and Beijing. He adds that from an economic perspective, internal migrations to cities are as important as international migrations.

Woetzel argues that when immigrants are considered costs, then they are treated as costs, and as such they need to be reduced. When cities reduce spending on immigrants, then—humanly speaking—migrants show a tendency to behave as costs and act as a burden instead of builders of a better community.

If, however, cities look at migrants as assets, or as people to invest in, communities may develop faster, become more productive, and repay the investment with higher productivity, which in turn will generate better outcomes for both cities and immigrants. Mayors in cities worldwide are taking action on inclusion issues at the grassroots level, which is a challenge faced primarily by cities (Woetzel, 2016).

International disruptions and migrations

The number of international migrants worldwide has increased steadily over the last 15 years. One of the causes of the phenomenon is greater global connectivity that allows people to learn about better conditions in other countries, encouraging them to relocate or seek asylum—an increasingly apparent force—and leave behind the native nation.

The number of international migrants grew from 173 million in 2000 to 222 million in 2010 and 244 million in 2015, according to the United Nations *International Migration Report 2015*, which presents data on human migration. This high level of mobility is disrupting nations and systems worldwide (United Nations, 2016). Box 3.1 illustrates the dimensions and challenges of human mobility.

Box 3.1 World migrations

Large-scale migrations 2010–2015:

- Europe hosts 76 million migrants, Asia 75 million, United States and Canada 54 million, Africa 21 million, Latin America and the Caribbean 9 million, and Oceania 8 million.

- In 2015 two-thirds of all international migrants were living in 20 countries.

The largest number of international migrants (47 million) resides in the United States. Followed by:

- Germany (12 million)

- Russia (12 million)

- Saudi Arabia (10 million).

- In 2014 the total number of refugees in the world was estimated at 19.5 million.

- Turkey was the largest refugee-hosting country worldwide (1.6 million refugees), followed by Pakistan (1.5 million), Lebanon (1.2 million), and the Islamic Republic of Iran (1.0 million).

- More than half of all refugees worldwide came from three countries: the Syrian Arab Republic (3.9 million), Afghanistan (2.6 million), and Somalia (1.1 million).

- Women comprise slightly less than half of all international migrants.

- The share of female migrants fell from 49% in 2000 to 48% in 2015.

- Female migrants outnumber male migrants in Europe and North America

- In Africa and Asia migrants are predominantly men.
- The median age of international migrants worldwide was 39 years in 2015, a slight increase from 38 years in 2000.
- But the migrant cohort is becoming younger in some regions. Between 2000 and 2015 the median age of international migrants declined in Asia, Latin America and the Caribbean, and Oceania.
- Most migrants worldwide originate from middle-income countries (157 million in 2015).
- Between 2000 and 2015 the number of migrants originating from middle-income countries increased more rapidly than from countries in lower income groups.
- The majority of migrants from middle-income countries are living in high-income countries.

Birth place of migrants:

- In 2015, 43% of the 244 million international migrants worldwide were born in Asia.
- 25% of migrants (62 million) were born in Europe.
- 15% of migrants (37 million) were born in Latin America and the Caribbean.
- 14% (34 million) were born in Africa.

Largest emigrations in 2015:

- India had the largest diaspora/emigration in the world (16 million)
- Mexico (12 million)
- Russian Federation (11 million)
- China (10 million)

- Bangladesh (7 million)
- Pakistan (6 million)
- Ukraine (6 million)

Positive net migrations:

- Between 2000 and 2015 positive net migration contributed to 42% of the population growth in North America and 32% in Oceania.
- In Europe the size of the population would have fallen between 2000 and 2015 in the absence of positive net migration.

Source: adapted from United Nations (2016)

Technological disruptions

Like previous industrial revolutions, this one has potential to raise global income levels and improve life prospects for populations around the world. But for this potential to be realized, it is necessary to pay special attention to social problems and increasing economic inequality.

To date those who have gained access to progress have been wealthier consumers with access to digital technology, and new products and services that increase efficiency and opportunities for pleasure. Ordering a cab, booking a flight, buying a product, making a bank payment or transfer, listening to music, watching a film, or playing a game, can now all be done remotely, something unheard of just a few years ago. Lower costs in accessing technology have significantly reduced the costs of transactions, opening access and opportunities to billions of new consumers worldwide.

For those who still do not have access to technology and connectivity, Google is developing an innovative global project called Loon for All or Balloon-Powered Internet for Everyone that is intended to connect people in urban and rural communities, worldwide.[1] Other technology start-ups are targeting similar markets.

The information revolution

The ways in which information and knowledge are shared are changing at a remarkable pace due to the well-documented advances in technology. There is a plethora of developments in information transfer that are affecting ways of working in business and education. One example that has moved from being viewed with some skepticism but is now regarded as an increasingly reliable method of sharing information freely and easily through crowdsourcing is Wikipedia.

For two and a half centuries and until the beginning of this millennium the sources of general information were bounded by the major encyclopedias. The Encyclopaedia Britannica, first published in Edinburgh, Scotland and the World Book Encyclopedia, published since 1917 in Chicago, Illinois, had been the principal sources of general reference.

In 2016 Amazon.com advertised the collection of 32 hard cover books of the 15th Edition of Encyclopaedia Britannica at US$421.[2] The price of the 24 hard cover books of the World Book Encyclopedia collection ranges between US$329[3] and US$1,000.[4] Pricing makes the printed versions of these encyclopedias a significant expense for

1   Loon for All YouTube presentation, https://www.google.com/loon/
2   https://www.amazon.com/Encyclopedia-Britannica-32-Book-Set/dp/0852299613
3   https://www.amazon.com/World-Book-Encyclopedia-2015-Volumes/dp/071660115X
4   http://store.worldbook.com/store/p/399-World-Book-Encyclopedia-2016.aspx

most people today in terms of money and physical space on book shelves.

An inquiry on the contributors of information to these encyclopedias chronicles that Britannica has "thousands of eminent experts, scholars, and leaders since the company's founding in 1768, that include more than a hundred Nobel laureates, four presidents of the United States, countless Pulitzer Prize winners and others of international renown".[5] Encyclopaedia Britannica also reports that contributors to the World Book Encyclopedia "include authorities in the physical, biological, and social sciences and other fields".[6]

But the beginning of the millennium brought about an information revolution ignited by the discovery of the wiki and Wikipedia, which disrupted traditional encyclopedias with the innovation and democratization of information contribution and readership followed by exponential growth in free and easy access to online technology and global connectivity.

A wiki means a brief idea expressed in a sentence that allows for collaborative modification of contents and structures. The wiki concept was invented by Ward Cunningham, a computer programmer. Originally it was an offline system he developed to track ideas flowing throughout his company. Cunningham coined his invention "WikiWeb" after he took a ride in the Honolulu airport shuttle bus, Wiki-Wiki. Wiki was the first Hawaiian word he had to learn in order to follow directions to ride the "Wiki-Wiki". "Wiki" means "quick" and Cunningham applied it to the WikiWeb as a very quick web.[7]

---

5   http://corporate.britannica.com/about/contributors/
6   https://www.britannica.com/topic/The-World-Book-Encyclopedia. This source provides no details about information contributors. Neither Google nor Wikipedia searches gave any results.
7   Ward Cunningham, Inventor of the Wiki, https://www.youtube.com/watch?v=XqxwwuUdsp4

In 2001 Wikipedia formalized wikis in the web, revolutionizing information as a free internet encyclopedia that allows users to edit (almost) any article on the site. It is now the largest source of general reference. It is ranked among the ten most popular websites in the world. Wikipedia is owned by the nonprofit organization, Wikimedia Foundation, which was launched by Jimmy Wales[8] and Larry Sanger, coining the name from *wiki* and encyclo*pedia*. Initially Wikipedia was only in the English language but quickly developed similar versions in other languages with different content. Wikipedia now contains more than 40 million articles in over 250 languages and reports 18 billion page views so far and nearly 500 million visitors each month.[9]

Wikipedia reports that the size of the community of contributors has shown exponential growth since the beginning. "In April 2008, writer and lecturer Clay Shirky and computer scientist Martin Wattenberg estimated the total time spent creating Wikipedia at roughly 100 million hours." At the time of writing,

> the English Wikipedia contains 5,325,800 articles which is the cumulative product of 29,924,396 registered editors and an unknown number of anonymous contributors. There are 117,615 active editors in the English project, a number that increases constantly. About half of the active editors spend at least one hour a day editing and a fifth spend more than three hours a day.[10]

8   Jimmy Wales: The birth of Wikipedia. Ted.com. July 2005. https://www.ted.com/talks/jimmy_wales_on_the_birth_of_wikipedia?language=en#t-74949

9   Wikipedia. The free internet encyclopedia. https://en.wikipedia.org/wiki/Wikipedia

10   Wikipedia contributors. https://en.wikipedia.org/wiki/Wikipedia_community

FIGURE 3.1 Wikipedia monument in Słubice, Poland

Figure 3.1 shows the Wikipedia monument in Słubice, Poland. Its inscription reads:

> With this monument the citizens of Słubice would like to pay homage to thousands of anonymous editors all over the world, who have contributed voluntarily to the creation of Wikipedia, the greatest project co-created by people regardless of political, religious or cultural borders.[11]

11 Wikipedia contributors. https://en.wikipedia.org/wiki/Wikipedia_community

As in any self-governing massive source of information, Wikipedia is not free from critics. In 2005 a BBC News article published details of Wikipedia achievements and areas of improvement, including a comparison with the Encyclopaedia Britannica (BBC News, 2005). Wikipedia fundamental principles for contributors are spelled out in "Five Pillars" accessible on its website.[12]

I need to add a personal note about Wikipedia. When I taught courses in Executive MBA programs during the last decade, I banned Wikipedia as a source of reference and any reference was marked with a minus in students' papers. Until a group of executive students came to me with to discuss this argument: *Professor, you are asking us to consult reliable references to discover new ideas to improve old business problems. But on one hand, most of us do not have access to academic journals because a) it requires subscriptions that are long term and expensive, b) most are highly theoretical and not easy to read or interpret, and c) do not foster creativity and innovation, you request from us.* I started to visit Wikipedia to understand the concerns of my students. We agreed on the use of Wikipedia not as the main reference, but as a complementary source of primary information on a specific subject. Executive students from other countries who spoke other languages made important contributions to the global dimension of many topics we covered in face to face and online classes researching local issues in Wikipedia. The free encyclopedia will continue growing and as more responsible contributors participate it will become a more reliable and global source of information always subject to improvement.

Global connectivity

In 2015 Huawei launched the Global Connectivity Index (GCI) in 50 countries to monitor advances and benchmarking in the digital

---

12   Wikipedia: Five pillars. https://en.wikipedia.org/wiki/Wikipedia:Five_pillars

economy transformation (Huawei, 2015).[13] The index shows usage of digital transformation including networks, computing, storage, service demand, e-commerce, and five enablers of digital transformation: data centers, cloud services, Big Data, broadband, and the Internet of Things.

The Index identifies which countries are best poised for development and growth based on ICT standards in the digital global economy. In 2015 the United States ranked first among 50 surveyed countries, followed by Sweden, Singapore, Switzerland, and the United Kingdom. Chile, China, and the United Arab Emirates (UAE) lead the ranking among developing markets. While developing country leaders have high levels of mobile adoption and digital access, compared with digital markets in developed nations they lag behind in data center investment and core elements of ICT infrastructure.

Cyber-vulnerability

The benefits of global connectivity expand in parallel with threats that increase ICT system vulnerability and require constant vigilance. Cyber threats are extremely agile, versatile, and difficult to detect even for the most conspicuous organizations worldwide.

Experts assess that information security is not exclusively a technical issue but it is overall a management challenge that rests on three foundations: critical digital infrastructures, organization, and technology. Although critical digital infrastructures are beyond the direct control of the organization, balancing them is a critical component of corporate governance.

Moreover, total IT security is not feasible or operationally practicable, so organizations must individually determine which information assets need to be protected and to what degree.

13   http://www.huawei.com/better-connected-world/en/

As internet-based commerce diffuses through society, customers will have decreasing tolerance for losses stemming from cyber vulnerabilities, in all kinds of organizations. In this environment senior management will be hard-pressed to deploy plans and policies effective in solving security threats in a balanced and integrated manner. Dutta and McCrohan (2002) state that leaving security primarily to IT departments may strengthen technology but will not yield intended results because cyber security problems are indeed management failures rather than technical fiascoes.

It is increasingly clear that innovations in technology will cause major disruptions in organizations in all sectors worldwide. But in contrast with past revolutions, technological transformation has greater potential for gains in efficiency and productivity if visionary leaders and organizations anticipate change, pursuing continuous learning and improvement to enhance agility and speed in managing and optimizing the outcomes of disruptions. For instance, education, health care, transportation, communication, global logistics, and supply chains can all become more efficient by increasing digitalization to decrease costs of production and delivery (Glatzel *et al.*, 2014). The costs of trade will then diminish, opening new markets worldwide and driving economic growth.

But there are also disruptions with potential to become significant threats; these must be recognized in advance to avoid the human costs seen in previous industrial revolutions.

Organizations and leaders need to be aware that technology changes can shorten the life span of ideas, business models, and market positions, forcing people and organizations to rethink the way they collect and manage information—or how businesses monitor and respond to competition—in order to turn disruptions into opportunities for reinvention, growth, and differentiation.

Moreover, communications technology must not displace people from the center of progress, as machines did in the past; technology is useful, but only if people can use it.

Disruptions affecting people

The Fourth Industrial Revolution will change what people do but also the essence of human beings. It will affect privacy, ownership, and consumption patterns, work time and leisure styles, careers, learning, skills, and how people meet and nurture relationships. Change is already evident in these areas, as it is in health, where "qualifying" data is becoming the norm, and the list will be limited only by human creativity.

Technology will generate benefits and costs that will become increasingly tangible over time. For instance one of the perceived costs is that integrating technology has serious potential to hinder communications between people, cooperation, and even compassion. Over-dependence on iPhones and constant connectivity can deprive life of values such as reflection, gatherings of family and friends, and engaging conversation.

Privacy will be increasingly curtailed by information technologies, as tracking and sharing information becomes an important component of connectivity.

This loss of control over personal data, scary as it is, will inevitably intensify in the future with the potential to redefine life span, health, cognition, and even moral and ethical values.

Disruptions of an aging population

The rapid growth of an aging population is currently largely overlooked and it has significant potential to introduce deep disruptions in education systems, industries, economies, and societies worldwide.

In the years after World War II, the world's population got younger because of increasing fertility rates and population growth in most countries, regardless of national income level. Improvements in health care, declining infant mortality, and increasing access to education have created a virtuous circle for a population that kept growing in sync with the working-age cohort that was fueling unprecedented economic growth.

Population growth brought significant benefits to societies worldwide, as more people and increased industrialization meant more demand for goods, services, houses, and schools that in turn generated more jobs and higher incomes for workers, and more tax revenues for governments. With the aid of technology, people work less and are more productive.

But in the 21st century the world is getting older and faster.

Little attention is given to the development of longitudinal studies necessary to make long-term economic and social forecasts. In many developed economies—plus China, the world's largest developing economy—people are living significantly longer and have fewer children.

Worldwide the baby-boom generation is older and entering retirement while fertility is falling sharply. These trends are reaching a tipping point and it is predicted that in the next few decades the world population will plateau for the first time in modern history (most likely with the exception of Africa). Developed and medium-income developing countries will have significantly larger proportions of older populations, aging workforces, and rapidly expanding expenses in social programs that will increase government expenditures to unprecedented amounts (Dobbs *et al.*, 2015).

Beyond demographics, technology is adding longevity to the trend toward an aging population, increasing life expectancy and helping people to live in healthier conditions. Next-generation genomics, a combination of sequencing technologies, big data analytics, and technologies that are able to modify organisms, will have the potential to increase human power over biology to cure diseases, such as cancer and cardiovascular maladies that are currently the most common killers in many places (Dobbs *et al.*, 2015).

Changes in demographics and disruptions caused by an aging population are trends that require special attention because they are deeply transforming management and the ways education, organizations, and society deal with elderly consumers, learners, employers, employees, stakeholders, and stockholders.

Here is some evidence of an aging world. In 1950, developed countries had twice as many children (15 and under) as older persons (65 and over); in 2013 older persons outnumbered children by a margin of 21% to 16%. If the current trend holds, by 2050 developed economies will have twice as many older persons as children (Dobbs *et al.*, 2015). The number of "superaged" countries (more than one-fifth of the population is 65 and older) would rise from three in 2015 (Germany, Italy, and Japan) to 13 in 2020, and to 34 in 2030. The impact on retirement systems is predictable and consequences are discussed in the section on government disruptions.

Disruptions in education: Building the talent society

Globally, education will play a far more significant role in the Fourth Industrial Revolution than in previous economic and social transformations. Educational systems and institutions unable to adapt to rapid change, adopting efficiency innovation and emerging technologies, will not only postpone change, but will become major barriers to progress. Hindering students' development and thus failing to match demands in labor markets will deter economic growth and expansion of inclusive societies.

In a constantly changing global environment, education systems and institutions need to find, develop, and deploy mechanisms to optimize the outcome of disruptions (Beer *et al.*, 2016). The discussion that follows identifies some of the fundamental principles necessary to build resilience and bridge gaps to solve management challenges, disruptions, and threats in education.

- Educational systems and institutions anchored in administrative process and management-by-objectives of the past must be disrupted by Human-Centered Management models focused on satisfaction of consumers' needs and expectations that lead to continuous improvement, quality standards, and increasing productivity and competitiveness.

- Human talent will increasingly substitute physical capital as the essential driver of economic growth.

- Forms of education unable to meet the demand for skills and talent in labor markets cause major disruptions in organizations and the economy, and are major obstacles to foster inclusive societies.

- Organizations exist to serve customers/users. Organizations in all sectors that ignore increasingly well-informed consumers are major constraints in attaining sustainability. Educational institutions are no exception.

- Organizations in the private and public sector must be problem-solvers for customers who buy or receive their products and services; otherwise they are problem-creators. Again, education is no exception.

- Educational institutions unable to identify and develop the talent of students, helping them accumulate human capital and organize knowledge to meet the demands of

21st century labor markets, will increasingly segregate the economy and society into "low-skill/low-pay" versus "high-skill/high-pay" and induce social unrest, segmentation, and inequality.

• Educators, education systems, and institutions at all levels will be increasingly disrupted by innovative and highly competitive educational institutions at all levels.

The measure of our ignorance

Economist Edward Denison (1962), who participated in the development of the monetary instruments to measure gross national product (GNP), acknowledged its limitations in assessing people's wellbeing a long time ago.

Denison (1979, 1985) called the large unexplained portion of the GDP "The Measure of Our Ignorance". Emerging measures of growth that include human and social development—over and above monetary accumulation—like national happiness indexes or national wellbeing reports, which are disrupting the actual GDP measurement system, are pressing development imperatives.

Education is the main sector responsible for talent development in the 21st century. As the world advances directly into the talent economy there are significant challenges to consider (Martin, 2014). On the one hand, there is a need for innovation at all educational levels, increasing articulation between different levels and robust integration between academic programs and emerging demands in labor markets.

On the other hand, the inequality of income between top talent and routine workers is a critical deterrent to sustainable economic growth, and one of the most insurmountable obstacles to attaining inclusive societies. Therefore solutions will depend extensively on the responsibility and capacity of educators and educational institutions.

Technology and automation will continue disrupting education and displacing workers, therefore anticipating disruptions will be the best strategy to diminish costs and increase benefits of disruptions in education and organizations (Davenport and Kirby, 2015).

Disruptions in labor markets

If human needs and safeguards are ignored during the Fourth Industrial Revolution, deep disruptions in labor markets will displace workers and increase income inequality, hindering human wellbeing and creating social unrest.

Focusing on Human-Centered Management helps to anticipate disruptions in education, organizations, and labor markets to avoid workers being displaced by new technologies. But to take advantage of disruptions in labor markets, educational systems at all levels— particularly higher education and academia—need to be aligned with emerging demands and we need to prepare students for the jobs of the future, instead of lengthening the lines of unemployment.

For the first time in history, human talent—over physical capital— will be the most critical factor of production. On the positive side, although every human being has talent and potential to develop it, education is one of the most important drivers for human capital accumulation, and particularly for people in lower income cohorts.

If education fails to assume responsibility for learners' learning, synchronized with personal needs meeting dynamic demands of labor markets, social inequality could become a most critical challenge to the Fourth Industrial Revolution.

Technology has displaced many lower-skilled workers in many countries across the globe, and increased demand for highly skilled workers, but with decreasing wages.

The talent economy will increase the volume of disruptions in labor markets, including growing numbers of disillusioned and fearful workers with diminishing wages and incomes. This explains why middle income groups around the world are now demonstrating a pervasive sense of dissatisfaction and unfairness towards a winner-takes-all approach for a few that offers limited opportunities for workers with less or inadequate education.

Falling fertility, slow population growth, and aging populations will have profound impacts on the labor force, organizations' productivity, and national competitiveness. New workers will enter at lower rates while older people will work for a longer time. The labor force age range is expected to expand from today's 20 to 65 to include workers in older age groups expected from 20 to 80 years of age and perhaps beyond, depending on health, living conditions, and need for income to survive in old age.

Based on recent trends, the annual growth rate of the global labor force declined 1.4% annually between 1990 and 2010 and it will contract 1% per year between 2011 and 2030. Worldwide the share of older workers (65+) in the workforce is expected to increase from 14% in 2010 to 22% by 2030. This change will be felt most acutely in developed economies and in China, where the share of older workers will increase to 27 and 31%, respectively, across the same intervals (Dobbs *et al.*, 2015).

Disruptions in business

Exogenous disruptions

Customer focus

Customers will be the epicenter of businesses confronting pressing demand for efficiency innovation and continuous improvement of products and services to meet quality standards of better informed consumers.

In an economy led by customers the consumer focus will generate new approaches to deal with increasing disruptions, including adopting new global platforms and business models that increase consumer demand for sophisticated products and services (Torres, 2016).

Innovation

Innovations supported by new technologies are changing consumer preferences and affecting competitive advantages, thereby disturbing traditional industries with global impact. Uber and Airbnb are just two examples of an exponentially growing entrepreneurial trend.[14] The Open University, founded in the United Kingdom in 1969 to provide higher education and academic degrees online, today serves learners around the world, revolutionizing the higher education industry.[15] In 2016 OU reported 2 million students with a truly global academic model, claiming to be flexible and reputable in meeting the needs of learners around the world.

Disruptions from agile competitors

Disruption is also flowing from the most agile and innovative competitors with easy access to global digital platforms for research, development, marketing, sales, and distribution with growing potential to displace well-established business organizations underscoring or postponing efficiency innovation and quality improvement (Valdez-Perez (2015).

---

14   Uber. Our story. https://www.uber.com/our-story/; Airbnb world rentals https://www.airbnb.com/
15   The Open University, http://www.openuniversity.edu/

Technology

Technology is shifting demands, providing high levels of transparency that facilitate consumer engagement and entirely different patterns of consumer behavior enabled by increasingly affordable access to mobile networks and connectivity.

Shifts in consumers' demands will disrupt companies and will press organizations to adapt and adopt new ways to design strategies and serve customers in emerging market segments.

Global business executives across industries show increasing concern over disruptions that are hard to anticipate and frequently surprise even the best connected and best informed leaders and managers (Enriquez and Smit, 2016).

All leaders conclude that technology is empowering the Fourth Industrial Revolution, disrupting demand and supply chains and forcing businesses to find new ways to do things (Turber *et al.*, 2015).

Clayton Christensen's disruptive innovation

The term "Disruptive Innovation" was coined by Harvard University professor Clayton Christensen in his 1997 book *The Innovator's Dilemma* to describe how an entrepreneur can develop a simple application that can take root at the bottom of a market and relentlessly move up eventually displacing well-established competitors.[16]

Christensen maintains that companies that innovate faster than their customers' needs evolve end up producing products so sophisticated and expensive that they are unattainable for many customers. He argues that companies that innovate within higher tiers of their markets—charging higher prices to the most demanding,

---

16   Clayton Christensen's Disruptive Innovation, http://www.claytonchristensen. com/key-concepts/

sophisticated, and wealthier customers—open doors for "disruptive innovation" by snubbing lower income consumers eager to buy cheaper alternatives produced by "disruptive emerging businesses" that produce and compete at the bottom of the market.[17]

On the supply side, disruptive innovation will be increasingly common in this fourth revolution, opening crucial opportunities for savvy entrepreneurs and smaller firms to enter new market segments (Dyer *et al.*, 2009). On the demand side, disruptive innovations are introducing a broad variety of products and services to meet different preferences and budgets, and are significantly decreasing their prices.

Resilience disruption

In 2016, two decades after Christensen popularized his book *The Innovator's Dilemma*, Joshua Gans (2016a, b), professor at the University of Toronto's Rotman School of Management and chief economist of the University of Toronto's Creative Destruction Lab, contended that resilience is the antidote for disruptions, and emphasized that some companies are more resilient than others to manage disruptions.

Gans looked at resilient companies and companies that have fallen behind. He explains that companies that are successful in managing disruptions depart from conventional business wisdom in two basic ways: demand and supply side. Companies fail in the demand-side when they focus so intensively on their main customers as to underestimate new market entrants offering innovations that target and disturb their demand niche. Keen attention to benchmarking and competition is advised to solve these disruptions.

17   Ibid.

Gans' Innovation Dilemma captures the need to innovate both internally with human talent and agility, and externally, expanding market niche. To this end he highlights three key factors: 1) an integrative organizational model; 2) production of products and services that are continuously important to customers; and 3) a strong sense of corporate identity (Gans, 2016a).

Disturbances and the speed of change are inducing a different dynamic in corporate longevity and sustainability that require increasing levels of resilience followed by innovation.

While in the 1950s the average S&P 500 US company remained in business for an average of 60 years, in 2011 average longevity was down to 18 years. At the current rate, and affected by increasing mergers and acquisitions, frequent fall of incumbent firms and a rapid rise in start-ups, estimates indicate that 75% of the S&P 500 of today will not exist or will be replaced in the next 10 years (Dobbs *et al.*, 2015).

Endogenous disruptions

Technology will displace the knowledge worker

There is ample precedent that technology and automation either force workers into higher level jobs—that machines cannot perform—or displace them from the labor force. The impact of disturbances caused by artificial intelligence are unpredictable, so it is almost impossible to envision the impacts on workers, organizations, the labor force, the economy, government, and society.

The outlook is worrying if technology and automation continue pushing away workers in general, but particularly the well-educated and highly skilled knowledge workers, identified by Peter Drucker in his book *Landmarks of Tomorrow* (1959).

Aging population will work longer

For the first time in history, five generations will be working side by side in organizations (Knight, 2014), introducing disturbances and generating new challenges to deal with a highly diverse workforce in terms of age, demographics, gender, and nationalities. Given that people will live longer while the returns on investments are decreasing, and government social security is debilitating, most people will need to work longer and delay retirement. Capelli and Novelli (2010) argue that today it is common to see someone younger supervising older people, which requires acknowledgement of potential tensions in multi-generation teams and the need to consider the age issue as an important element in leading and managing organizations.

Klaus Schwab illustrates one of the multi-generational challenges in the workforce as follows:

> The millennials, a generation born digital, are completely at ease with technology and will have a much stronger impact on social behaviour than we currently assume. As they enter the workforce, they represent a huge engine of transformation for every institution—public and private.[18]

Gender issues and demand for flexible work schedules

The work-life balance policies originally designed in the 20th century to support working mothers and female caregivers with flexibility, will continue in the 21st century.

Nonetheless sharing home and work responsibilities remains a challenge for professionals of all genders who prefer occupational flexibility; this will create particular disruptions in business organizations seeking diverse and talented workers regardless of gender or marital status (Southworth, 2014). Offering company

18   Klaus Schwab, Founder and Executive Chairman, World Economic Forum, Opening Speech, World Economic Forum India Economic Summit 2010, New Delhi.

options helping them to lead happy, healthy, and more productive lives will be important factors that will contribute to improving workers' performance and productivity.

Multinational workforce

Increasing global migrations are changing the face of businesses and organizations, disrupting traditional structures and requiring multi-cultural and multi-language capacities to meet the needs of an increasingly international mix of workers. In itself, this mixture is required in order to satisfy increasingly global clienteles. Amazon and Alibaba are just the beginning of a wave of fast growing global commerce.

Disruptions in government

Technology, transparency, and citizens' engagement

Technology and accompanying new platforms will allow citizens to engage with governments in different ways to access services, voice complaints, and coordinate actions.

Overall, technology will diminish the central role of government and will transfer power to people, either through public engagement or through the decentralization of functions with new sources of distribution powered by technology.

In turn, technology will also give governments power to expand the digital infrastructure and increase surveillance of populations based on security imperatives. Privacy will be increasingly volatile.

Safety and surveillance

The role of government will increasingly be influenced by the capacity to face disruptions from structures that provide high levels of transparency and efficiency to maintain a competitive edge.

Stagnant government agencies will face mounting trouble and public discontent, particularly in the regulation sphere of public policy and decision-making built on outdated regulatory frameworks of processes designed to be linear and follow strict hierarchical approaches.

The Fourth Industrial Revolution will challenge legislators and regulators to unprecedented levels; first, serving the interests of consumers and the public at large who embrace freedom, change, and innovation (Wales and Tretikov, 2015). Second, governments will have to address the agility imperative to build versatile governance, just as the private sector has to do in order to remain productive and competitive.

Furthermore, governments and regulatory agencies will need to collaborate closely with business and the civil society to expand opportunities for business and trade growth that foster development.

The Fourth Industrial Revolution will have profound impacts on the nature of national and international security affecting the probability and nature of conflict. The differences between war, peace, and violence, including cyberwarfare, will become increasingly blurred. But advances in technology also have the potential to reduce the scale and impact of violence with new modes of protection (Hillis, 2013).

The welfare state and 21st century massive aging population

Longer life expectancy of the world population and lower investment returns will leave the elderly less able to retire without significant assets (Dobbs et al., 2015). Dramatic changes in demographics—fewer people working and more people receiving retirement—will balloon budget deficits, forcing governments to boost the retirement age and or privatize social security systems (Kritzer, 2005).

Among 31 countries that in 2015 had established private mandatory individual retirement accounts (IRA), Chile was the first to do this, in 1981 (*ibid.*). Countries that have followed the Chilean privatization model include Bolivia, the Dominican Republic, El Salvador, Kazakhstan, Argentina, Colombia, Peru, United Kingdom, and Uruguay (*ibid.*).

Aging populations and government retirement programs will create increasing disruptions in governments in European countries with compulsory state pension systems where the welfare state is highly visible. Large countries that concentrate the bulk of the European Union's population and GDP, such as France, Germany, Italy, and Spain and others with unfunded retirement systems will require major adjustments of public budgets to avoid financial clashes and social unrest. Exceptions to this include the UK and The Netherlands (that have large private pension systems), Sweden and Poland (that have introduced IRAs), and others with sound public finances able to finance government retirement systems with tax revenues.

Growing disruptions will come from young generations resenting the confiscation of increasing proportions of their earnings and a rapidly growing number of retirees who live in constant fear of expanding budget deficits and the possibility of benefits cuts.

Europe is aware that the budget of government social welfare depends on fertility rates and life expectancies. But at this stage both are inconsistent with the demographic megatrends of the 21st century.

Massive migrations into Europe may postpone or increase the problem because immigration of low-paid workers or lack of language skills can exacerbate unemployment rates and reduce wages, diminishing collection of payroll taxes. Although immigrants pay taxes during their working lives, they will also collect retirement benefits.

Therefore immigration may postpone the European welfare state and pension fund dilemma but government budgets will have to aggregate expenses accrued by support programs for immigrants from other regions of the world (Piñera, 2004).

If Europe intends to maintain prosperity and ensure peace for its citizens it will need to evaluate the costs and benefits of moving toward a comprehensive retirement system based on ownership, individual freedom, and individual responsibility for retirement funds (Piñera, 2004).

Potential benefits of disruptions

Klaus Schwab (2016) expressed special concern about organizations unable to adapt, governments failing to deploy new technologies to optimize benefits, emerging security concerns, and segmented societies with increased inequality.

At the heart of his analysis is a conviction that the Fourth Industrial Revolution is controlled by people who need to be aware that global collaboration, across sectors and disciplines, is essential to grasp the opportunities it presents.

In particular, Schwab (2016) and Lepeley et al. (2016) call attention to the importance that leaders and citizens working together *affectively* and *effectively* can shape a common future in which putting people first and empowering human beings are constant reminders that new technologies are tools developed by *people to help people*.

Schwab (2015) states that exogenous disruptions can be manageable because human beings have the capacity to manage their impact through their daily decisions as citizens, consumers, producers, or investors.

The main challenge for people, organizations, and governments is to grasp opportunities that can shape the Fourth Industrial Revolution, directing them toward a future where humans are at the center of progress, and change reflects human values and common objectives.

Challenges can be more difficult sometimes, not because people are incapable, but because decision-makers are trapped in traditional thinking and linear strategies and absorbed by multiple crises that demand their attention, conflicting with the challenges at hand.

Schwab (2016) ends his WEF presentation by stating:

> In the end it all comes down to people and values. We need to shape a future that works for all putting people first and empowering them. In its most pessimistic, dehumanized form, the Fourth Industrial Revolution may indeed have the potential to "robotize" humanity and deprive us of our heart and soul. But as a complement to the best parts of human nature—creativity, empathy, stewardship—it can also lift humanity into a new collective and moral consciousness based on a shared sense of destiny. It is incumbent on us all to make sure the latter prevails.

Part II

Four (of the five) pillars of Human-Centered Management

Part I discussed the driving forces that position human beings at the center of management and organizations in the "Age of Knowledge", the global economy and interconnected societies.

Although the imperative is that life on earth improves when all human beings can attain wellbeing, few realize that all people, individually and collectively, are responsible for this outcome. Furthermore, people have full potential to improve themselves and the institutional environments that contribute to making life better. But commonly limited access to quality education (education for life), lack of skills, experience, and a visionary outlook drive people to distort, deteriorate, and even destroy organizations and environments when faced with unfavorable circumstances.

Based on the disruptions identified in previous chapters, the speed and breath of change, and the challenges ahead, the rest of the book presents a Human-Centered Management model to support quality-driven people and organizations seeking high performance, competitiveness, and sustainability around the world.

The uniqueness of the Human-Centered Management for Quality Sustainability HCMxSQ model that contrasts with other efficiency-seeking methods is its positioning of people (instead of processes) at the center of the quality imperative, as the focus of attention, and responsible for their own well-being, the organization's success, and, in turn, accountable for their individual and collective contribution to national ESTE Balanced Economic Growth (economic, social, technology, environment) required to attain inclusive societies.

The HCMxSQ organization is built on a matrix structure led by a people-centered constructive governance and long-term work teams responsible for the mission, principles, and ethical values projected to customers and the community, offering products and services developed by human capital and resilience that transforms disruptions of the global VUCA (volatile, uncertain, complex, ambiguous) environment into opportunities for innovation and continuous improvement.[1] The organization structure is supported and strengthened with strategies designed by agile networks of talented individuals responsible for managing change and responding rapidly to customers' needs and external demands across all the units in the organization.

Four pillars are focused on the development of essential elements of Human-Centered Management: 1) human capital; 2) disruption resilience; 3) talent management; and 4) agility. The fifth pillar discussed in Part III is a comprehensive quality assessment model to objectively measure that the organization attains the continuous improvement required to demonstrate quality standards in order to attain sustainability in the 21st century.

---

1   The 2016 5th Ashridge International Research Conference. *AIRC5 Global Disruption, Organizational Innovation.*

Framework of the Human-Centered Management for Organization Quality and Sustainability (HCMxSQ)

Human-Centered Management: The 5 Pillars of Organization Quality and Sustainability

Organizations

Structure:
(hardware)

Mission, vision, values, identity, planning

Teamwork (long term)

Strategies:
(software)

Change, innovation

Networks (short term)

HC Management

1. *Human Capital*

2. *Disruption Resilience*

3. *Talent Management*

4. *Agility*

HC SQ Management

5. *Sustainable Quality Model*

- 7 Management Areas

- 35 Assessment Elements

Quality Cycle & Scoring:

- *performance evaluation*

- *continuous improvement*

- *sustainable quality*

4

Pillar one: Human capital

Challenges and opportunities

The human capital concept was developed by Gary Becker (1930–2014), an American economist and professor at the University of Chicago and Fellow at Stanford University. Becker received the Nobel Prize in Economic Sciences in 1992 for his pioneer contribution to developing the human capital theory as one of the most important missing elements of economic development and growth.

To most people, capital means a bank account, investment in corporate stock, government bonds, production, or steel plants. Although each of these are forms of physical capital, in the sense that they are tangible assets that over time pay yields and increase income—or decrease it—people also accumulate intangible assets.

In his book Human Capital. A Theoretical and Empirical Analysis with Special Reference to Education, Becker (1993) argues that all the intangible assets a person accumulates throughout life, such as education, good health, and virtues like honesty, ethics, commitment, and punctuality, help to consolidate a better, happier, and more productive life.

Personal wellbeing in turn also provides benefits to others: family members, friends, and to the organization where the person works. Personal wellbeing increases productivity in organizations, contributing to economic growth and a more inclusive society.

Becker called human capital an intangible asset, meaning that it cannot be detached from the person who owns it. People cannot be separated from their knowledge, skills, health, or values as they can from tangible or financial assets. This is a crucial difference between physical capital and human capital. While physical capital can increase or decline, personal human capital is maintained and must be updated when knowledge becomes obsolete.

Gary Becker together with Theodore Schultz (1902–1998), his senior colleague at the University of Chicago who also won a Nobel Prize in Economic Sciences in 1979, conducted extensive research which positioned education as one of the main resources a person can access to accumulate human capital.

In his book *Investing in People: The Economics of Population Quality* (1982), Schultz stresses the requirement that people seek continuous education throughout life. He also highlights the importance and responsibility of educational institutions to provide learners with relevant and useful education to comply with their social responsibility to help all students advance in life, beyond getting good grades.

Regardless of whether students attend private education—where they pay directly for educational services—or public education, financed through taxes paid by populations and companies and administered by governments, all the producers of education (schools, colleges, and universities worldwide) are responsible for delivering quality education. Namely, education that meets the needs and expectations of learners, their families, and the demands of labor markets that condition improvement or deterioration of the economy and society.

Failing to live up to educational responsibilities hurts all incumbent students and it is an irreparable waste of time and resources. This is a fundamental principle until now not properly understood or followed, largely because education has historically been a *supply-driven* industry, where consumers are forced to adapt and accept whatever educational services educators and institutions provide, as freedom to choose has rarely been available.

Schultz and Becker built an important legacy about the urgent need to offer and receive quality education. However, they were writing several decades ago, and although education is as critical today as it was then, the positive effect of education on people has consistently declined, mainly because the speed of change in both the global economy and the development of technology are fast, deep, and dramatic, while education lags behind the demands of learners and of labor markets. This is a worldwide phenomenon.

In 2012, Richard Florida, professor at the University of Toronto's Rotman School of Management and New York University, disturbed audiences worldwide when he announced that society is in the midst of a fundamental economic and cultural shift led by an emerging cohort of people that he denominates as the **Creative Class.**

Florida argues that human creativity is the pivotal force of economic and societal change. Most importantly he emphasized that every human being is creative and it is time to harness the power of human creativity across society.

Florida called attention to the imperative to universalize creativity as an antidote to increasing inequality. To this end he proposed the "Creative Compact" built on six central principles (Florida, 2012b):

1. Invest in developing the full human potential and creative capabilities of every single human being

2. Make openness and diversity and inclusion a central part of the economic agenda

3. Build an education system that spurs, not squelches, creativity

4. Build a social safety net for the creative economy

5. Strengthen cities; promote density, clustering, and concentration

6. From growth for growth's sake to true prosperity: measure what really matters

His proposal is important and irrefutable when he refers to the shortcomings of education. The *growth for growth's sake* that Florida refers to is an old concern. I came across this misdemeanor in the 1980s while conducting research for my economic thesis on human capital. Edward Denison, one of the scientists who participated in the design of the GDP formula to measure economic growth in the United States (physical capital + labor + land), had expressed serious concerns about the shortcomings of economic analysis that excludes human capital variables. Denison (1979) accurately coined the unexplained portion of the GDP as "The Measure of Our Ignorance".

Denison wrote Trends in American Economic Growth in 1985, and in spite of growing controversy and recurrent objections regarding the critical limitations of the instrument. Today many economists and policy-makers continue to use the obsolete GDP formula to conduct studies and allocate resources, naturally leading to misleading results.

Florida's principle on the need to reduce inequality resonates in Human-Centered Management. It is important to clarify that HCM proposes to increase equality, instead of reduce inequality, because these concepts have different meanings.

One school of thought proposes to reduce income inequality, blaming market systems for increasing income gaps in the Gini coefficient.[2] Instead, Human-Centered Management favors a different line of action, making human beings responsible for the ethical—or unethical—behaviors that drive markets: this is based on the view that markets are nothing more than an instrument moved—or obstructed—by people.

HCM respects and promotes human freedom and favors markets as the most effective instrument known until now to improve human life, expand trade, decrease costs of products and transactions, and expedite distributions of goods and services to populations.

HCM is supported by individual and collective responsibility for the improvement of organizations and the economy, and low levels of government intervention in markets, stressing that successful deployment of this responsibility is highly correlated with access for all to quality education.

It is concentration of power—and not markets—to blame for economic imperfections that lead to social failures and unequal income distribution. Power concentration of any kind, in the private or the public sector, constitutes a major interference with people's wellbeing and is the cause of free market distortions that destabilize markets and increase income inequality.

Income inequality is the result of education inequality

One of the most critical factors determining income inequality is inequality in education. Although this correlation is emerging and does not have extensive exposure, it will be increasingly important in development.

---

2   National index that measures income distribution disparities among citizens.

The works of Schultz and Becker sent a strong signal to international development organizations (United Nations, OECD, the World Bank, etc.) and to developed and developing countries about the need to increase investment in education to increase economic growth and development.

Education is the Achilles' heel of economic growth and social development. Educational challenges are surmountable based on evidence that increasing investment and access does not result in human capital accumulation unless education offers quality standards and meets the needs of all students it serves. Inequality in education is the most important determinant of income inequality.

After studying this problem extensively I found that the main obstacles to improving education are rooted in the following causes:

- When the structure of the industry is supply driven

- When educators are reluctant to change at the same speed as the times and where unions present powerful obstacles for change based on students' imperatives

- When educators and institutions are risk-averse, adhere to the status quo, avoid innovation, and lack the entrepreneurial spirit necessary to advance in the 21st century

Contrary to all other 21st century industries, educators and educational institutions are commonly penalized—instead of prized—for creativity and innovations, by bureaucratic and hierarchical systems embedded in rigid norms and regulations, highly centralized and detached from for students, parents, labor markets, and society.

Soft Skills: the strong core of human capital and Human-Centered Management

Educational planning is generally done looking at the past as in a rear-view mirror. Most educational institutions and systems still base quality yardsticks on student's grades and testing, underestimating fundamental Soft Skills, abilities, and knowledge that students need to succeed in life and the labor force in the 21st century.

There is a growing body of literature about the need for Soft Skills, which are also referred to as social or people skills at school level, in higher education, and business education in countries around the world (Lepeley and Albornoz, 2013; Bardy and Massaro Bardy, 2013; Majluf, 2016; Tarr and Weeks, 2016). There is growing awareness that Soft Skills are required to increase the human capital of the workforce. At the present time, when the most pressing challenge for organizations is how to increase productivity of work teams, it is not enough for schools to focus exclusively on academics, as people and students need to develop social skills and emotional strength, including self-management, self-awareness, and social responsibility.

Slowly but surely things are moving towards the Soft Skill model proposed by the authors mentioned above and expanding to new sectors and segments of education.

Awareness on the subject is shown in the article "Rethinking college admissions" based on a Harvard University project that "could make real difference because it nails the way in which society in general—and children in particular—are badly served by the status quo" and shows the need to develop Soft Skills to enter and survive in college and the workforce. The project, that the *New York Times* reports has the growing support of admission deans and other leaders of top US colleges and universities, is intended to "promote ethical awareness among aspiring students emphasizing that intellectual engagement is as important as ethical engagement to fairly assess the strengths of students across income, race, and cultures" (Bruni, 2016). Another article proposes to raise Soft Skills to the top of the education discussion (Weissbourd and Jones, 2014).

Mark Greenberg, professor of Human Development and Psychology at Penn State and co-author of the study "Improving Classroom Learning Environments by Cultivating Awareness and Resilience in Education" (Jennings *et al.*, 2013), stressed in an interview with *The New York Times* that the ability to get along with others significantly increases mutual empathy among students and between student and teachers, who reap more benefits from the classroom experience. Greenberg confirms that teaching Soft Skills to students builds over time like a cascade, helping students become more closely bonded with peers and experience reduced social risks (Bornstein, 2015). In spite of the fact that this is not a new insight, the results of a national survey show that 90% of schoolteachers consider it important for schools to promote the development of students' social and emotional skills, but most teachers are unprepared, and struggle to integrate these because they are rarely integrated in curricula (Tarr and Weeks, 2016).

The worldwide need for the development of Soft Skills is growing exponentially. Surveys I conducted among executives of corporations and organizations that have won the National Quality Award in Chile show significant deficit of Soft Skills among new hires (Lepeley and Albornoz, 2013). Similar results are observed in business schools in Italy (Bardy and Massaro, 2013) and in the US workforce (Tarr and Weeks, 2016; Lepeley *et al.*, 2016). This confirms an important gap that education must resolve, because it is hindering the development of the human capital that students need to succeed, and organizations demand to compete.

The search for the perfect team study conducted by Google supports this discussion. Researchers from one of the largest and most progressive innovators in technology in the world conducted "Project Aristotle", interviewing over a hundred Google teams with the aim of identifying the characteristics of the most effective teams that consistently delivered the best results. The findings highlighted two particular behaviors shared by good teams, which differentiated them from the control teams. First, team members showed significant respect for each other, demonstrating this through their awareness of providing equal participation and speaking time to all. Second, good teams showed high "social sensitivity", meaning that all members were highly skilled at inferring how others felt by their tone of voice, expressions, and other nonverbal clues and were respectful of these moods (Duhig, 2016).

Human capital investment

Human capital at school level

Students and families who have options to choose the educational institution their children attend are best positioned to access the best education because they can compare alternatives and pick programs with quality standards. Therefore freedom to choose one's educational institution is the best option to help students get the best education.

Freedom of choice in education stimulates *constructive competition* between institutions, necessary to foster innovation and improvement by synchronizing individual needs with an educational plan relevant for learners.[3] This is particularly important

---

3   *Constructive competition* is the positive and ethical way to attain continuous improvement observing others and benefiting from good deeds. It launches a virtuous circle to serve as a role model of high performance and provides incentives to induce improvement in the education, the community, and the

because today, with open access and the internet, parents and students have unprecedented opportunity to compare information about school performance to select institutions, programs, and instructors.

On the other hand, students and families restricted by government policies to attending schools in certain neighborhoods must accept the *supply-driven education* offered by public institutions that commonly have few incentives to innovate and improve.

Imposing education on parents and students becomes increasingly controversial when parents have options to compare but not to choose the best education for their children.

Parents of school children becoming better informed—independent of income level—is a growing trend with significant potential to increase the demand for quality standards in education, thus meeting the critical need to optimize human capital accumulation from an early age.

Human capital and higher education

Colleges and particularly research universities were traditionally the most important producers of human capital in society. But more recently corporations have created universities that better meet their human capital demands for quality education to increase innovation, productivity, and competitiveness.

Higher education programs are lagging behind the demands for human capital from the labor market. Colleges are increasingly unable to meet the needs for human capital formation among younger generations, millennials, Generation Z, iGen, and post-millennial students, who are highly connected and well informed about education alternatives with greater potential to help them

nation. The opposite is destructive education, where the purpose is to destroy competitors often using unethical means and privileged information.

enter the workforce and succeed at work, instead of getting a diploma to hang on the wall.

In Chapter 1 I identified famous college dropouts of the 20th century who, like Microsoft's Bill Gates and other emblematic cases, started the most successful technology companies. Many of them are among the wealthiest persons in the world, based on their self-made human capital.

Ironically the technology these people developed has deeply transformed higher education, introducing intense competition. And this trend will continue. Online education is revolutionizing the delivery and universalized open access to learners as never before. But as previously stated, increasing access to education is a good thing, but the most critical aspect is the quality of education that learners receive, allowing them to maximize their human capital and the rate of return on investments in terms of time, effort, and money.

Human capital at the corporate level

In addition to the disruptions that technology has introduced through online education, corporate universities are impacting higher and executive education enrollments. When higher or executive education supply deviates from and ignores the demands of the labor force, increased growth of corporate universities is expected and significant (Lepeley *et al.*, 2016).

The speed of change in the economy requires continuous training of an organization's personnel to retain and improve competitive advantages. Many corporations worldwide have universities to train employees. This is because on the one hand enrolling employees in university programs has become increasingly costly for corporations, and on the other hand employees trained in university programs fail to increase productivity as organizations expect.

Additionally, few organizations and corporations that invest in external training are effective in assessing the costs and benefits of learning to ensure that the human capital gained by employees supports the knowledge base and skills the organization needs. Few organizations instrument systematic assessment of employees' learning and how the knowledge employees have gained is shared to benefit others in the organization.

Continuous assessment of the results of external training programs is necessary to optimize returns on investment in human capital in alignment with the organization's demands. It is recommended that organizations select external training programs for employees based on employees' talent and interests, aligned with the organization's demands; also that they conduct follow-up assessments of effectiveness and efficiency, targeting specific areas that have been improved in the organization. This is necessary to synchronize personal with organizational human capital gains financed by the organization. (Lepeley *et al.*, 2016).

Human capital and migrations

There are global issues and challenges that affect individuals, organizations, and human capital accumulation and migration. Global standardization of work is one among the most pressing human capital challenges. Global mobilization of labor is today inevitable.

While some countries and regions accrue significant economic benefits from human capital due to immigration of *brain gains*, others suffer considerable losses of human capital due to brain drains.[4]

---

4   Brain drain refers to the outflow or emigration of well-educated and highly skilled people commonly—but not necessarily—from developing countries, who emigrate mainly for economic reasons, but increasingly due to turmoil in the native country (Lepeley and Albornoz, 2013; Lepeley *et al.*, 2016).

The economic implications of human capital migrations have multiple effects. *Brain gains* are favorable for nations that receive educated immigrants from other countries; commonly professionals from developing countries seeking better professional and economic opportunities. *Brain drain* is extremely detrimental for countries, and it is exacerbated in developing countries affected by social and economic turmoil that drives emigration of highly educated and skilled cohorts, thus hindering recovery.

Although people have migrated around the world since the beginning of humankind's history, recent massive migration is an unprecedented phenomenon that remains to be understood.

Today it is increasingly evident that developed and developing countries will continue constructing barriers to avoid the entry of low skilled workers, with the exception of demands in specific labor markets, commonly agriculture.

Ignoring the fact that migrations are prompted by human needs—including sheer survival in regions of conflict—people will continue risking their lives in search of better life opportunities. This is a human capital dilemma that deserves increasing attention because labor mobilization and resultant *brain gain* and *brain drain* have considerable effects in labor markets in both developed and developing countries.

Human capital and the global labor force

The world is changing as a result of human migrations. As labor movements become global, national differences tend to fade and labor laws, policies, and practices tend to standardize in response to migrations, corporations responding to changing demands in global labor markets, and negotiations of trade agreements.

Global corporations are a major force pressing for standardization of the workplace in terms of performance, quality standards, subjects related to employees' rights and responsibilities, health care, and pension systems that can be modified so that workers in all nations enjoy similar treatment and fringe benefits can be mobile. This is already the norm at executive level in most global corporations.

As trade agreements increase worldwide, government policies will press for standardized workplace norms and countries seeking to maximize economic growth will enforce strategies to attract human capital. In parallel, companies are increasingly prepared to operate globally and compete for human capital on a worldwide basis, as a historic source of competitive advantage.

On the topic of competitive advantage, the driving forces have shifted from organizational reliability and capital investment to human capital investments, innovation, and flexibility. To advance this transition and strengthen organizations in innovation and effective management requires an effective combination of the right structure and the right human capital.

Human capital optimization requires high levels of coordination and cooperation among employees, constantly bringing in new talent and technological expertise, with an unequivocal focus on talent management, disruption resilience, agility, and efficiency innovation leading to the continuous improvement and quality standards necessary to attain sustainability.

A unique human capital strategy for each approach provides the foundations for creating competitive and innovative organizations.

5

Pillar two: Disruption resilience

The second structural pillar of quality-driven organizations is Disruption Resilience.

In Chapter 3 I discussed major disruptions with the potential to impact management and organizations. In this chapter I discuss the role and importance of resilience as a structural antidote to deal with disruptions and accrue more benefits than costs from investments in human capital, change, and global connectivity that affect people and organizations worldwide.

The discussion examines the potential benefits of resilience at the personal and organizational level, emphasizing the need to synchronize personal and organizational resilience to optimize opportunities to transform disruptions in continuous improvement and innovation.

What is resilience?

The question is valid because the original concept referred primarily to the reaction of physical objects to external forces. Most recently it has been applied in psychology, and in this millennium it has been adopted by management and organizations.

The Merriam-Webster Dictionary defines resilience in objects as the "ability of something to return to its original shape after it has been pulled, stretched, pressed, and bent". And in people, as the ability to "become strong, healthy, and successful after something bad has happened".[1]

Resilience has commonly been associated with disaster and crisis management. It has been applied to people who survive adversity or suffer traumas and can adjust to new circumstances.

For the purpose of Human-Centered Management, resilience is the capacity of people to empower themselves and improve their lives, by developing capacity to help others and become agents for change and continuous performance improvement in organizations.

Personal resilience as pre-condition for organizational resilience

Resilience is not a natural organizational trait. Organizations become resilient because they have been successful in nurturing resilient leaders and employees. Therefore resilient people are a necessity for developing resilient organizations. In turn, organizations with a resilient labor climate can more easily attract and retain resilient and talented people.

---

1   Merriam-Webster Dictionary online. http://www.merriam-webster.com/dictionary/resilience

Personal resilience

Daine Coutu (2002), in a *Harvard Business Review* article entitled "How resilience works", identified basic principles of resilience that were later associated with organizations. Coutu, a psychologist, was an observer of people's behavior and the resilient capacity of certain individuals induced her to investigate the following queries: why do some people suffer real hardships and not falter? What is the essence of resilience that carries people through life? She concluded that although resilience is one of the greatest puzzles of human nature, in times of rapid change and mounting turmoil it is increasingly important for individuals and organizations to learn about resilience and how to build resilience at personal and organizational levels.

Academic research on resilience started in the 1960s with pioneering studies by Norman Garmezy, professor of psychology at the University of Minnesota. Today, theories about resilience abound. Studies conducted by Maurice Vanderpol, former president of the Boston Psychoanalytic Society and Institute, showed that many healthy survivors of concentration camps had what he calls a "plastic shield", which comprises several factors, including sense of humor, ability to form attachments with other people, and possession of an inner psychological space that protected them from intrusions of abusive agents.

The Search Institute, a Minneapolis-based nonprofit organization focused on resilience and youth, found that resilient children have an uncanny ability to get adults to help them.

Early theories of resilience also stressed the role of genetics: some people are born resilient. Coutu argued that there is some truth in this but she found empirical evidence that resilience can be learned. Her study on adult development conducted at the Harvard Medical School in Boston reported that within various groups studied during a 60-year period, some people became markedly more resilient over their lifetimes (Coutu, 2002).

Coutu found that all resilience theories overlap in three ways: a) facing reality; b) search for a meaningful existence; and c) ingenuity. A person can bounce back from hardship with one or two of these qualities, but is truly resilient with all three. Coutu states that these three characteristics hold true for resilient organizations as well.

Table 5.1 presents a summary of Coutu's resilience construct and the three overlapping ways she identified.

TABLE 5.1   Coutu's resilience construct

Facing reality	Search for meaning	Ingenuity
Resilience stems from an optimistic nature. Resilient people have down-to-earth views of reality and what matters for survival.	Ability to see that reality correlates highly with propensity to find meaning in tough times. Capacity to devise constructs about difficult situations that create new stimulating meaning for themselves and others. Capacity to build bridges from present-day hardships to a fuller, better constructed future. These bridges make the present more manageable and remove the sense that the present is overwhelming. Resilience is finding meaning in one's environment. Resilient people and organizations possess strong value systems. Resilience is not ethically oriented. It is merely the capacity to be robust under conditions of significant stress and change.	Ability to create something with whatever is at hand. Capacity to bounce back better and rebound stronger learning from obstacles. Improvisation in unpredictable times.

In her *HBR* article "What resilience means and why it matters", Andrea Ovans (2015) revisited Coutu's theoretical resilience model and added an interesting practical dimension based on results of a survey conducted by Bond and Shapiro on 835 employees from public, private, and nonprofit firms in the UK. The study identifies the *biggest resilience drains and gains* among employees in organizations. The biggest resilience drains at work, regardless of position, level of responsibility, or division in the organization, are shown in Figure 5.1.

FIGURE 5.1   **Biggest resilience drains at work**

Source: Author's table including data taken from Bond and Shapiro in Ovans (2015)

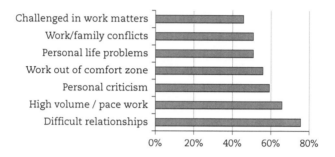

Figure 5.2 shows where people gain strengths to build resilience in organizations. The most cited sources were first, personal capacity to rebound, second, relationships, third, their work, and last the organization.

FIGURE 5.2   **Where do I get my resilience from at work?**

Source: Author's table including data taken from Bond and Shapiro in Ovans (2015)

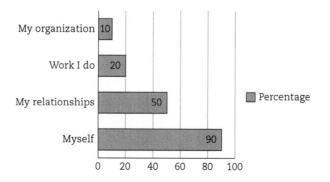

Ovans cites Farson and Keyes' (2002) arguments about the benefits of positive learning experiences to argue that leaders can create constructive working environments where setbacks and successes are both treated as positive experiences and, by breaking down social and bureaucratic barriers that separate them from the people they supervise, by showing personal engagement with the people they work alongside, including the capacity to acknowledge personal mistakes and avoid judgmental postures when they interact with employees.

Furthermore in *Building Resilience*, University of Pennsylvania psychology professor Martin Seligman (2011), a pioneer in positive psychology, also argues that business leaders can help employees become more resilient. He mentions the Penn's Resiliency Program where he teaches students to think positively about setbacks in order to build resilience. The university offers the UPENN Authentic Happiness Questionnaire that—to a certain extent—also serves to assess personal resilience.

There is consensus among scholars that the most important asset of organizations is their employees and building resilience is increasingly necessary to help employees face disruptions and constant change (Sheffi, 2005; Van der Vegt *et al.*, 2015). Resilience training, including cross-training and shifting assignments in organizations, can help employees develop adaptability and flexibility. This also helps employees to switch jobs more easily and become resilient, adjusting to disruptions during peak operation times.

Communicating clearly and explicitly to employees the organization's strategies, identifying hurdles and discussing initiatives to move forwards with operational processes, current status, results, areas of improvement, cash flows, and inventories, are important elements to develop resilience by keeping everybody on the same page and avoiding costly duplications.

Empowering employees to take action to develop resilience by building on effective communications allows them to strengthen efficiency and agility. Since a large portion of the investment in people involves training, team members trained to adapt quickly to new circumstances can respond faster to fluctuations and unexpected disruptions, thereby accruing more benefits for stakeholders and the organization.

In the context of disruption management, certain instances of hectic environments can help organizations manage disruptions more efficiently and get better results from resilient behaviors (Sheffi, 2005).

Van der Vegt *et al.* (2015) identify a series of individual characteristics, skills, abilities, cognitions, affects, behaviors, and self-regulatory processes that help to build resilience. Among them are intelligence, self-efficacy, emotional stability, openness to new experiences, social support, emotion recognition, self-discipline, resourcefulness, and cognitive flexibility. The authors emphasize that systems with greater diversity of individual characteristics better withstand disturbances, responding in a variety of ways. In terms of teams, they find that personalities and abilities relate closely to the capacity to work together. An adequate composition of individual characteristics may determine the system's potential for resilience, while relationships between individuals and social network determine how the collective can offer responses when people are engaged and willing to advance purposeful actions (Van der Vegt *et al.*, 2015).

Mastering individual resilience is necessary to respond to complex and unpredictable disruptions and change in organizations. But the transformation to a resilient organizational culture requires *constructive leaders* who recognize and reward people's ability to bounce back from disruptions, not only as an organizational challenge but as an experience of personal growth. Constructive leaders know how to differentiate between strengthening resilience in people and the organization, and the perils of creating buffers to ignore disruptions and avoid change, which invariably increase individual fragility and organizational vulnerability.

Organizational resilience

Yossi Sheffi (2005) in *The Resilient Enterprise: Overcoming Vulnerability for Competitive Advantage*, argues that some organizations respond to disruptions better than others, not because their processes are fundamentally different, but because there is something "in their DNA" (Kindle, location 2509 of 3543) that is conducive to agile response and change.

He defines resilience as the ability of an organization to bounce back from disruptions. Interestingly, he states that to develop resilience a company does not only need to have a security department, but "a 'risk manager' whose responsibility is to build capacity to recover and, most importantly, isolate customers as much as possible from organizational disruptions."

Sheffi (2005) says that building organizational resilience requires agile process management and frequent redesign of operations, transformation of organizational culture, changes in product and service design, different relationships with customers, personnel, and stakeholders, and constant analytical consideration of disruptions and risk factors.

Given the positive dimension emphasized by Coutu (2002) and Ovans (2015), and the personal effects on resilience identified by Van der Vegt *et al.* (2015), it may be inferred that people can enhance—or hinder—the positive dimension of resilience in organizations. The purpose of this inference is not necessarily to emphasize that a positive attitude can be a remedy for all menaces, but rather that a negative attitude is a spontaneous and snap reaction, and it takes great effort and courage to transform negative feelings into a positive output.

To build resilience requires changes and adjustments in people's perceptions about the way to do things that invariably impact the organization. Change requires increased agility to gain capacity to conduct systematic assessment to monitor decisions, actions, operations, and results.

Some operational processes will need to be redesigned to meet customers' expectations and bring about change. Deployment of systematic assessment of outcome takes time and experience, but once it is achieved, systematization decreases work significantly, improving products and services in organizations working to develop optimal relationships with customers, personnel, and stakeholders.

To assess an organization's resilience, monitor progress, and design interventions for improvement it helps to design a **disruption map** with two characteristics: 1) identifying whether disruptions are internally or externally induced; and 2) listing disruptions in order of importance. This map must be simple to ensure that it can be regularly updated by everybody involved.

Fiksel *et al.* (2015) in a *Harvard Business Review* case study entitled "From risk to resilience: learning to deal with disruption", refer to the importance of monitoring disruptions constantly, as globalization has made anticipating disruptions and managing them increasingly challenging.

They assess that the structures of settled and stable corporations are more vulnerable during disruptions because most lack the agility strategies necessary to react, respond, and move forward quickly. They also caution against a tendency among companies to focus on the supply side at times of disruption, underestimating attention required by the customer side and the demand side, pointing out that this shortcoming hinders recovery in the short run and improvement in the long term.

Fiksel *et al.* (2015) assess that companies that rely too heavily on risk identification at a time when many of the disruptions are unpredictable, or depend highly on statistical information, can receive more harm than help from risk forecasting and stats.

Fiksel *et al.* (2015) developed Supply Chain Resilience Assessment and Management (SCRAM), a framework to assess the order of vulnerabilities that make organizations susceptible to disruptions that can jeopardize the capacity to anticipate and overcome them. SCRAM helps companies identify important supply-chain vulnerabilities and areas that need to be strengthened, including network diameter, network clustering, and network hierarchy, which are each important determinants of network resilience. Based on their work with companies like Dow Chemical, Johnson & Johnson, and Unilever, they emphasize the need for an assessment framework that enhances resilience capabilities.

Van der Vegt *et al.* (2015) argue that resilience is particularly relevant in supply chains which are the backbones of organizations and businesses in the global economy.

Disruption Resilience®

Organizations seeking to optimize performance, productivity, and competitiveness have to pay special attention to building a resilient climate because happy and satisfied employees contribute to all of the above.

Moreover, the results of the Bond and Shapiro (Ovans, 2015) study showed explicitly that employees cite the organization as the last resource to seek personal resilience, giving a low score to the organization's capacity to build and maintain a resilience climate at a time when the importance of resilience in people and organizations becomes much more relevant to confront frequent and unavoidable disruptions.

Disruption resilience is a commitment—not an option—for organizations seeking to optimize benefits and minimize the costs of disruptions. In this case, resilience is the capacity to transform work into a source of personal satisfaction for those involved in the organization, where workers feel appreciated doing something meaningful and consistent with their expertise and efforts to attain continuous improvement. When work is a burden, a restraint, or an obligation it obstructs individual performance and organization sustainability.

6

Pillar three: Talent management

Companies and countries will compete for the best and the brightest. Talent scarcity is driving the growth of an internationally mobile creative class that encompasses five generations of workers. Competition for talent will come not only from the company down the street, but also from the employer on the other side of the world. It will be a seller's market, with talented individuals having many choices. Both countries and companies will need to brand themselves as locations of choice to attract this talent (World Economic Forum, 2011).

The third strategic pillar in quality-driven organizations is talent management.

What is the difference between human capital and talent management?

Many ask me this question. Although they may seem similar, there are critical differences that must be clear to understand causation. Human capital has been an important concept in economics, and particularly in development economics since Gary Becker won the Nobel Prize in Economic Sciences for his pioneering theories of human capital in 1992. Talent management is a development of the 21st century.

Return to investment in human capital

The following analogy explains in simple terms one of the most complex *complements* in economics and management.

Human capital is equivalent to the money a person has in a savings account. Talent management is equivalent to the investment strategies the account owner—or an agent—follows to get the highest possible return on the investment of the money in the savings account.

In the knowledge economy, talent is the core of human capital.[1] Although every human being has some kind of talent, supply-driven education is not an effective agent to identity the talent of students. On the contrary, it often obstructs students' creativity, essential to develop and strengthen personal talent.

Do you know your talents?

In the leadership training program I teach, I ask participants to list at least five talents they have in one minute. Only a few complete this requirement on time. Most people are not aware of their talents, and are therefore unable to strengthen nature's gifts.

At an individual level, talent is a set of abilities and aptitudes a person possesses that are useful to perform activities, solve problems, and find solutions that generate personal benefits and utility (Meyers *et al.*, 2013). At the collective level, talent is the sum of individual talents that endorse and strengthen organizational performance, productivity, and competitiveness.

---

1 Also called the **talent economy**.

Talent management is the capacity of organizations to anticipate and effectively fulfill the responsibility to identify people's talents and train them to improve themselves first, and in turn contribute to improving collective performance, productivity, and competitiveness.

Talent evolution

In ancient Greek culture, talent was the name of the unit of measurement of precious metals. In the 21st century it became increasingly evident that the talent of people was a critical factor in successful organizations.

McKinsey, the corporate consulting company, introduced the talent concept to management, conducting an extensive study on talent in 1997. Talent studies continued and in 2010 the book *The War for Talent* (Michael *et al.*, 2010) revealed that, contrary to the traditional assumption that talent management (TM) should be under the supervision of the human resources division, TM is the responsibility of visionary leaders able to discover talent in people and select the most suitable training program to help individuals to improve and in turn help the organization. The study emphasizes that this kind of leadership is the most significant element that distinguishes high performing and quality-driven organizations from average performers.

Talent management requires talent strategies

To develop talent management strategies, organizations need to be aware that TM cannot be left solely to the HR division but must be the constant responsibility of visionary leaders at all levels of the organization, from executives to line managers and subordinates in all divisions.

TM strategies include but are not limited to: discover, attract, train, develop, retain, promote, and advance all employees in the organization to continuously expand the talent pool.

The effectiveness of TM strategies must be assessed periodically to observe the degree of alignment of the talent of people in the organization with the outcome of operations, production, customers' satisfaction, continuous improvement, performance, productivity, cost structures, revenues, and market demands.

TM strategies of employee evaluations include measurement of *current performance* and also *future potential*. *Current performance* refers to the employee's capacity to meet organizational responsibilities consistent with personal traits, level of knowledge, hard and Soft Skills, and experience required to succeed in the job, and *future potential* is based on personal creativity, ingenuity to innovate, and other skills the employee is capable of using to increase his or her level of responsibilities relating to improvement of the organization.

Talent management and sustainability

Although in most organizations TM is not yet a priority, the increasing volume of disruptions is pressing TM to the forefront in a rapidly growing number of businesses and organizations. TM was not a priority in the industrial past, but in the 21st-century knowledge and information age, lack of TM strategies is a highly hazardous omission for organizations because human capital has surpassed the importance of physical capital as the main driver of growth and sustainability.

TM takes precedence in quality-driven organizations, helping employees to optimize performance, strengthening competitiveness and returns on investments, and setting blueprints for innovation in customer service, new products, and Constructive Leadership to attain global success.

Organizations started to think about human talent when the Father of Management, visionary Peter Drucker (1959), coined the concept of the knowledge worker. The concept gained importance with McKinsey's studies and other research. Among others, Randall Schuler (2015), another important pioneer researcher in TM, correlated visionary leadership with talent management in his article analyzing what companies are doing to manage talent for the last decade.

Schuler emphasizes that organizations increasingly consider people's talent as the most valuable asset. He also links talent with leadership, organizational culture, and effective coordination of internal strategies with the external environment and the community, using analytical tools and techniques that are understood and supported by everyone.

Schuler assesses that integrating TM into day-to-day practices is achieved by prioritizing the explicit purpose of excellence and agility to serve the interests of all organization stakeholders and shareholders in the short and the long term.

Based on global research in corporate assessment, Schuler developed a 5-C framework where he identifies, organizes, suggests, and documents many choices (Cs) for managing talent used by global companies, regardless of country of origin. The 5 Cs for managing talent are: Choice, Consideration, Challenges, Context/ Contingencies, and Consequences (Schuler, 2015).

TM is a widely discussed management topic in academia, among consultants, senior executives, and managers. Furthermore, leaders managing talent or practicing talent management (TM) or global talent management (GTM) argue that TM is no longer a choice but is mandatory to succeed and excel.

To manage talent effectively requires leadership and careful choices because decision-making is a much tougher responsibility with the speed of change and the diverse nature of disruptions that affect organizations, where there is always more than one set of policies and practices to achieve success.

Managing organization talent

McKinsey proposes the following five universally accepted TM strategic initiatives to improve performance (Brüggemann *et al.*, 2015). The first four focus on enhancing individual talent and the fifth targets organizational and collective talent management.

1. Attract and recruit talented people with compelling stories to manage talent in the organization

2. Train and develop employees based on holistic learning and cross-company imperatives

3. Provide support to employees to become well-rounded leaders and workers at every organizational level and offer well-defined career paths

4. Reward employees effectively based on specific and diverse performance measurements and improvement incentive systems

5. Foster connectivity across the entire company with dedicated cross-functional initiatives

It is important for organizations to develop awareness to find innovative formulas to develop TM to continuously increase the stock of human capital.

In the book *Treat People Right! How Organizations and Individuals can Propel Each Other in a Spiral of Success* (2003), Edward Lawler III, one of the leading change management experts in the United States, shows that organizations that "treat people right" have higher chances of becoming highly productive and competitive, getting the highest rates of return on investments in human capital.

Lawler draws a TM formula that includes the following elements:

- Ensuring not only good working conditions and good pay, but building special relationships where individuals and the organizations are synchronized to create synergic processes, high performance, and continuous improvement, generating benefits for individual employees, the organization and all the stakeholders

- To attain these goals the organization must have the capacity to keep employees satisfied and constantly motivated to improve performance, projecting an identity that attracts high achievers, supports high achievers, and supports regular employees to become high achievers

- Leadership that enhances talent management and integrates and promotes continuous improvement values and actions in the short and long term across the organizations (Lawler III, 2003).

Talent and creative environments

Dul *et al.* (2011) propose effective articulation of creative personalities within the social, organizational, and physical work environment under the supervision of TM and the people management office to develop creative environments that enhance performance in the workplace.

Dul *et al.* (2011) state that the knowledge workers, or "the creative class" (Florida, 2012a), are core elements for organizational competitiveness in the knowledge economy, because these employees lead the creation, distribution, and application of knowledge to such an extent that their talent becomes as important an asset in production as was previously emphasized in human capital. Their talent generates high returns on investment in human capital with useful ideas and solutions for products, services, and process renewal.

Because people's creativity depends not only on their personal talent but also on their social and physical work environment, organizations can promote creativity by focusing on these aspects. Other strategies include encouraging employees to take risks, eliminating fears of failure (Birkinshaw and Haas, 2016), stimulating the exchange of ideas, and allowing employees to try new solutions for old problems. Organizations can support leaders to motivate employees to be more creative by offering explicit acknowledgment and rewards. There is an abundant body of research findings confirming that physical work environment enhances creativity and organizations can use it to their advantage.

A creative model for talent development

Dul and Ceylan's (2011) creative environment proposal is displayed in Figure 6.1. This organizational environment identifies the elements and articulates a formula to support and enhance people's creativity and job satisfaction, using their talent to increase performance in organizations.

FIGURE **6.1** **Proposal for a creative work environment**

Source: Dul and Ceylan (2011)

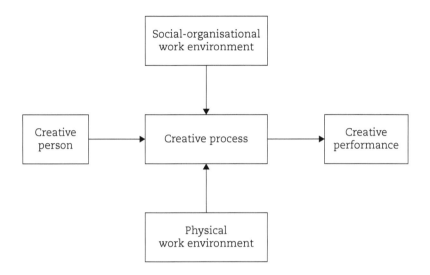

Manage your talent to maximize returns

Concluding the TM chapter, although we are in the era of knowledge and the internet, TM is one of the most important assets for human capital accumulation within organizations. The growth of individual and collective talent depends on efforts to develop agile and effective strategies for progress and to avoid becoming an obsolete organization siloed in the status quo and an unstimulating environment.

7

Pillar four: Agility

Agility is the fourth strategic pillar of quality-seeking organizations.

Why agility in organizations?

A *disruption resilience* strategy is necessary for organizations to recuperate from shocks, setbacks, and disruptions with greater capacity to *adapt* to and *adopt* change. Agility is a perfect complement to disruption resilience and it is imperative for organizations to manage change effectively, innovate, and move forward to continuously improving quality standards and sustainability (Rigby *et al.*, 2016).

Recurrent concerns in Human-Centered Management are complex work environments where people get overwhelmed with the speed of change, find competing priorities hard to manage, and there are obstacles to adjusting to change.

Change commonly has negative impacts on people, performance, and productivity (the 3 Ps) when it is not properly managed. In most organizations the speed of change is an unprecedented experience, so many organizations lack capacity to adapt fast enough or do not have reliable guidelines to follow; situations that increase operational costs and threaten organization sustainability.

In the global VUCA (volatile, uncertain, complex, ambiguous) environment even when personal work priorities seem clear and manageable, new disturbances emerge that shake off certainty and affect all stakeholders.

On the external front, better informed customers are pressing organizations with increasing frequency for more products and services, faster and better delivery, and demanding quality standards as never before. Competition induced by technology is increasing exponentially and innovation in all industries is the norm in the marketplace.

Internally, organizations' old techniques are failing to meet new challenges. Diverse demands and impositions (including external regulations) are constantly shaking the status quo, while demand for products and services grows faster. Organizations that confront these mounting challenges using traditional means of production hinder operations and growth potential.

To adjust and respond effectively, organizations need to adopt agility strategies as an inclusive framework for continuous improvement and avoid segmented efforts that in the long run increase costs of adjustments and postpone the attainment of quality goals. For instance, avoid putting all organizational agility responsibility in just a few talented people, and avoid improving agility in just a few processes. The experiences of organizations in developed and developing countries show that the shortcomings of piecemeal interventions to develop agility jeopardize organizational success and have significantly higher costs than efforts to deploy a comprehensive agility strategy.[1]

---

1   I have observed businesses and organizations that have won National Quality Awards but over time fail to keep up with an agile and holistic approach

What is agility?

Personal agility

Definitions:

- Personal physical agility: ability to move quickly and easily [2]

- Personal mental agility: capacity to think quickly and clearly

- Corporal body agility: ability to change positions efficiently and integrating different movements combining balance, coordination, speed, reflexes, strength, and endurance. [3]

Where:

- **Balance**: ability to maintain equilibrium when stationary or moving with coordinated sensory functions

- **Coordination**: ability to synchronize movement of all the functions

- **Speed**: ability to move all or some parts of the body quickly and easily

- **Reflexes**: ability to respond instantaneously to stimulus

- **Strength**: ability to overcome resistance

- **Endurance**: ability to be resilient and adaptable and remain active for long periods of time

Agility synonyms: Mindful, quick-witted, resourceful, ready, brilliance, imaginative, sharp, acumen, artful.

---

to continuous improvement to support change in leadership and fall behind standards of performance excellence.

2   Cambridge Dictionaries
3   Wikipedia

More definitions:

- **Business agility**: capacity to move quickly to respond to customers and take advantage of market conditions to gain competitive advantages

- **Management agility**: organizational approach to do things, understanding that making changes when needed is key to continuous performance improvement

Organizational agility

In the book *The Agility Factor: Building Adaptable Organizations for Superior Performance,* Worley *et al.* (2014b), three recognized American scholars in organizational effectiveness, define "agility not only as ability to change, but as the accumulated capacity that enables organizations to respond instantly, effectively and in a sustainable way when changing circumstances require". Worley *et al.* (2014a, b) emphasize that agility is strategically important for organizations not only for the sake of change, but to focus on improving performance and competitive advantage.[4]

Agility is a central development in management. It evolved to help organizations turn from the traditional, inward-looking focus on bureaucratic and predictable environments, to an outward-looking awareness necessary to respond quickly to disturbances.

Agility is a critical management strategy in outward-looking customer and market-oriented business organizations that deploy quality management. The need for agility draws much attention in software companies pressed to develop agile techniques to solve problems quickly and innovate for increasing competitiveness.

---

4   Christopher Worley, "What is agility?" CrossKnowledge YouTube Videocast. https://www.youtube.com/watch?v=-ArKdlonMig

To deal with challenges and solve complex problems with agility, software companies noticed that teamwork was initially unpredictable, but when team members became flexible, teams could reach identifiable patterns of good performance (Duhig, 2016).

The high turmoil environment of technology companies provides evidence that despite high levels of unpredictability, agile people can develop agile organizations best positioned to take advantage of competitive environments.

Agility is becoming the modus operandi in increasing numbers of organizations in diverse industries, ranging from start-ups, to entrepreneurial business, corporations, non-profits, government agencies, and community organizations.

Advancing from traditional to agile organizations: Not only teams but also networks

Lawler and Worley (2006), in the book *Built to Change: How to Achieve Sustained Organizational Effectiveness*, showed that to succeed in the global economy, organizations need to be agile. They contend that in the 21st century, organizations that perform like a Swiss watch, constantly repeating the same behavior, obstruct change and build vulnerabilities to confront disruptions. Organizations, they argue, need to have structures and strategies to deal with change and stimulate innovation. To this end, Worley and Lawler state that organizations need to be closely connected to their external environments—customers, markets, the community—and be aware of the agility of the internal environment, rewarding employees for experimentation, new practices, new technologies, and strengthening commitment to continuous improvement.

Agility—both physical and mental—is a human trait. Agility in organizations is inherently rooted in interactions between people and social networks that define the modus operandi in agile organizations.

Consequently, to build agile organizations it is critical to understand people's interactions as exchanges among individuals who work and collaborate, hold a common vision, possess the necessary resources, and show a diversity of behaviors, abilities, and diverse experiences that complement each other to facilitate collaboration to advance the organization's mission of consolidating its identity.

Human beings are an essential driver in agile organizations, because new ideas, solutions for improvement, and new products emerge from people and are strengthened in organizations through human interactions. A single agile person has limited power to impact on an organization's overall agility, because it is human interactions and networks, beyond a single individual, that provide the drive which leads to change and progress in agile organizations.

Resilient teams and agile networks

At this point it is important to define the differences between teams and networks to operate quality-driven organizations.

Resilient teams are formed by a group of persons who work in the organization with the purpose of developing long-term projects, programs, or plans. Resilient teams are responsible for performance, productivity, and development and for spreading resilience across the organization.

Agile networks are spontaneously organized groups of people from diverse divisions and levels of responsibility who *volunteer* to form short-term networks with the objective of planning innovative projects and extrapolating ideas with the potential to benefit the organization through the development of products or services that will increase the organization's competitiveness.

Networks are formed by free thinkers: compulsive learners who brainstorm ideas wherever they find them and adapt them ingeniously to solve problems in the organization.

Networks are constantly monitoring the external environment, aware that once products or services are launched there will be immediate reactions from customers and competitors, with great potential to force new changes. This never-ending cycle in organizations is resolved with agility and effective management to conquer competitive challenges.

Networks—in contrast with teams—can move faster under high levels of uncertainty and ambiguity. Such tensions are necessary, as they help to keep network members alert, and organizations open to valuing change and chaos as pre-states for innovation and improvement, not as upheaval or turmoil.

In terms of agility assessment, it is common to hear managers claim that their organizations are agile. Probing deeper reveals that agility is narrowly defined and circumscribed to the design of a new product or a fast response in certain areas of production. It is less common to hear agility associated with human interactions, networks, or accumulated capacity to respond to changing circumstance that impact organizations.

Agility in organizations was a central subject in the 2016 World Economic Forum when discussing the concerns over the Fourth Industrial Revolution in terms of the speed of change and unprecedented impacts on people, business, and organizations worldwide.

Current events have transformed the common management question: why is agility important in organizations? Now, managers are asking: what is the best way to become agile?

Organization agility assessment

The organization agility survey shown in Table 7.1 is a sample adapted from the original developed by the Center for Effective Organizations (CEO) at the Marshall School of Business, University of California.[5] CEO is made up of a group of world-renowned researchers who create data-based knowledge and turn it into practice to support change in organizations worldwide (Worley *et al.*, 2014b).

Agility assessment: From inward to outward-looking organizations

To evaluate agility, organizations need to assess a balanced combination of inward–outward focus.

Organizations are founded on two fundamental principles: first, the *outward-looking* principle to respond to the needs of customers and market demands—in economics known as the "demand side"—which actually provides the reason for organizations to exist. Second, the *inward-looking* focus is based on optimal operations that produce products or services, or the "supply side". To accomplish the inward-focus, organizations hire and retain people who provide knowledge and talent in exchange for a salary.

5   https://ceo.usc.edu/

Table 7.1   Agility assessment: Organization agility profiler survey sample, CEO – USC

Q	Traditionally this organization …	Strongly disagree	Disagree somewhat	Agree somewhat	Strongly agree
1	… has a unifying purpose or mission other than profits and growth	1	2	3	4
2	… spends a lot of time thinking about the future	1	2	3	4
3	… encourages innovation	1	2	3	4
4	… considers ability to change an organization strength	1	2	3	4
5	… develops strategies thinking in flexibility	1	2	3	4
6	… puts most employees in contact with customers and the external environment	1	2	3	4
7	… provides a diversity of resources to stimulate people to improve products, services, or better ways to work together	1	2	3	4
8	… has a significant capacity to change	1	2	3	4
9	… the workplace embraces change as normal	1	2	3	4
10	… allows information to flow freely from the outside to units and groups where it is most valuable	1	2	3	4
11	… has flexible budgets that respond fast to market changes	1	2	3	4
12	… rewards performance more than seniority	1	2	3	4
13	… has core values that reflect a change-ready organization	1	2	3	4
14	… is transparent and shares financial and business strategy information with employees	1	2	3	4
15	… is capable of shifting its structure quickly to take advantage of new opportunities	1	2	3	4
16	… pays for training and people's development that contribute to improve performance	1	2	3	4
17	… systematically assesses learning from change efforts	1	2	3	4
18	… has formal mechanisms to connect executives with people at all levels of the organization	1	2	3	4
19	… encourages managers and supervisors to show leadership skills to be imitated across the organization	1	2	3	4
	Sub totals				
	Total score				

Survey scoring: circle number 1 to 4 in each corresponding category. Add each column. Add rows to get the total score. Scores closest to 76 points indicate a higher level of organization agility. Lower scores identify areas of improvement to increase agility.

Source: Center for Effective Organizations, University of Southern California

The perfect complement to inward–outward operations is a balance between a high-performing, all-inclusive structure with continuously improving operational strategies.

To organize operations, organizations develop a structure and strategies where the level of agility varies. Studies show that agility is lower in large, inward-looking hierarchical organizations with bureaucratic structures, centralized power, a high degree of control, and where employees are restricted by rules and regulations.[6] An inward-looking focus is characteristic of large organizations of the industrial past, which aimed to attain high levels of production, supplying machines in large quantities to meet growing demand amid minimal competition.

Outward-looking customer focus organizations started with Edwards Deming and total quality management (TQM) in the 1980s, as was discussed in Chapter 2. Organizations had to become more agile to satisfy growing numbers of customers and increasing competition with quality standards.[7]

Deming's TQM model gave origin to National Quality Awards programs in many countries, with the aim of providing a model that could help businesses and organizations in all sectors to increase performance, national productivity, and international competitiveness.[8] The globalized economy and free trade agreements are bringing organization agility to the forefront.

6   Bureaucratic organizations were designed by Max Weber (1864–1920) a German sociologist and political economist in his book *The Theory of Social and Economic Organization* in response to rapidly expanding markets for manufacturing products and it was a model that has prevailed since the Industrial Revolution along with Frederick Taylor's Scientific Management. Revise Chapter 2 on management evolution.

7   Japanese auto manufacturer Toyota was the first example of total quality management deployment in organizations around the world.

8   See details on National Quality Award programs discussed in Chapter 2.

The experience of quality award organizations worldwide shows that the most agile organizations have outward-looking *entrepreneurial structures*, simpler lines of production, matrix organigrams, expedite decision-making, are highly responsive to customers, and adapt quickly to market demands to remain competitive and be sustainable in the long run.

That the transition to the agile paradigm takes time and that new models to develop agility and attain sustainability are urgently needed cannot be ignored.

Agilizing the agility transformation

The transformation of a conventional organization with hierarchical structures into a matrix framed "shared responsibility" agile organization is a lengthy process with both tangible and intangible costs and constraints. Therefore, different options for this transformation must be assessed to select those that minimize costs and maximize benefits.

For some entrepreneurially focused organizations, advancing agility may be easy to achieve. But for large organizations the effort required from staff, and the costs of transformation can be high, so an alternative is to establish a Dual System Model.

Switching the organization's core structure (equivalent to the hardware) is difficult and takes time. So it is recommended that the transformation is begun by developing strategies (equivalent to the software) to make the organization more responsive—agile—to both internal and external improvement exigencies. To this end a parallel system or dual system model is a feasible solution.

The Dual System Model (DS) was developed by John Kotter, a professor at Harvard University, in his book *Accelerate: Building Strategic Agility for a Faster-Moving World* (2013). I recommend DS over other options because it enables organizations with older bureaucratic-hierarchical structures to achieve necessary flexibility using strategies that lead to agility.

DS consists of the development of a parallel system of agile strategies integrated with a traditional organizational structure. The new system introduces approaches that strengthen resilience and agility to foster continuous improvement and innovation. The original system carries on the organization's identity, mission, vison, values, and trustworthiness, which are worthwhile to maintain.

As it was previously emphasized, Kotter confirms that visionary leaders are essential to deploy DS in organizations. He defines visionary leaders as persons who can see beyond the obvious and have the courage to undertake risks to try new things that may change and improve the organization. His vision strengthens the **Constructive Leadership** framework of the HCMxSQ Model, which is described in the following chapters.

Kotter contends that in an ideal world there should be many visionary leaders in any organization and emphasizes that visionary leaders can be trained. He highlights that most people have capacity to be creative; the problem is that organizations lack cultures of creativity and originality, overlooking opportunities to discover visionary leaders.

Visionary leaders—and workers with potential—are agile, have a forward-looking vision of the organization, are enthusiastic, risk-takers, and possess empathy that empowers them to empower other people and serve as role models for quality and agility.

Organizations should consider that visionary leaders may or may not be part of the organization's upper echelons and should be mindful of including people who may hold lower levels of responsibility in other divisions of the organization.

Deployment of a dual system does not necessarily restrict, but may support the original structure, by making it more flexible. So in general it is not recommended to hire new people to advance the DS transformation, but to use the talent of visionary people who work in the organization, who volunteer their participation and show commitment to working in a different way. Volunteering commitment to change—in contrast with being designated to work on change—is a critical element in consolidating a successful DS because it implies a desire to do things differently.

In spite of evidence that people can change when they learn a better way of doing things, Kotter states that most organizations are designed for stability, not for change. Hence the "dual operating system", may be a *hand in glove* model to make organizations more agile.

In agreement with Kotter, Adam Grant (2016) in his HBR article "How to build a culture of originality: Anyone can innovate if given the opportunity and the support" emphasizes that organizations tend to believe that innovators are a rare breed. But indeed most people are quite capable of original thinking when they work in organizations that promote a culture based on innovation, social values, and human creativity.

Grant warns that senior managers and supervisors often fail to recognize creativity and originality because they think that their main responsibility is to control processes and operations, in the belief that these methods lead to better work. Although this mantra worked in the past in static bureaucratic organizations, it is obsolete and counterproductive in the 21st century.

Organizations need to give leaders and employees reasons to generate—and recognition for generating—lots of new ideas as a safe way to increase agility, embedded in a continuous search for improvement. To accomplish this objective Grant recommends creating networks of innovators who evaluate ideas proposed by employees and direct the discussion of potential success based on making balanced choices between traditional and innovative approaches, aiming to improve and strengthen the organization.

Agility and lean organizations

Goethelf and Seiden (2013), in their book *Lean UX: Applying Lean Principles to Improve Users' Experience*, emphasize that customers must be the focus of all organizations. They clarify that *lean*—slender, thin, simplified—strategies include principles, tactics, and techniques that teach from the ground up to experiment with new ideas with significant potential that need to be validated with customers' feedback.

Lean management is based on assumptions to maximize **customer value** while minimizing waste, creating more value for customers and an organization's stakeholders while using fewer resources.[9]

In lean organizations, value for customers must increase continuously, minimizing production defects. To accomplish this objective, lean thinking changes the focus of management from segmented use of technologies, assets, and vertical departments to optimizing the flow of products and services throughout an integral stream flowing across technology and assets across the organization to satisfy customers' needs and demands. Focus should be on eliminating waste across the organization instead of at isolated points, continuous assessment of processes using less space, less capital, and less time to make products and services with fewer defects. In this environment, information management becomes simpler and more accurate when compared with traditional organizations. Lean management responds to customers' changing desires and provides a variety of options.

Lean management built into collaboration among teams and integrated with agile networks to drive new designs in short and iterative cycles helps to safeguard what works best for the organization and its customers.

---

9   Lean Enterprise Institute definition.

Teams and networks use ingenuity and agility to advance toward continuous improvement. In lean management the design of a framework to stimulate creativity includes the following characteristics:

- Design initiatives to develop agility in people and across the organization, because although departments independently may value agility, interconnections with people in other departments may be uncommon or inefficient

- Frame a vision of problems and focus the attention of people in teams and networks toward creative solutions

- Share insights early and long before processes are in place

- Assess improvement continuously to ensure that ideas are valid and reliable

- Work to help employees become more productive, providing more and better ideas that improve efficiency so they can work better and work less, avoiding duplication and waste

- Develop capacity to continuously identify areas of improvement

- Understand organizational adjustments and shifts necessary to attain continuous improvement in processes across the organization

- Incorporate the voice of customers throughout the stream and project cycle

Graphic representation of structural transformation

Figures 7.1 and 7.2 illustrate the differences between the characteristics of traditional hierarchical and matrix organizations. Figure 7.1 shows a drawing of a traditional, inward-looking, hierarchical structure where a boss draws the organigram of an organization, housed in a sturdy building of the industrial past.

FIGURE 7.1   **Structure of inward-looking bureaucratic organizations**

Figure 7.2 shows a dual system where the core structure is managed by leaders and teams reorganized around a triangular structure powered by agile strategies.

The agile system is constantly evaluating strategies that lead to performance and results in congruency with an organization's mission, vision, and goals. This may be through adjusting technology and communications channels, or using employees' talent pools for optimal operations to deliver the products and services that customers demand.

FIGURE 7.2   Structure of outward-looking matrix dual system organizations

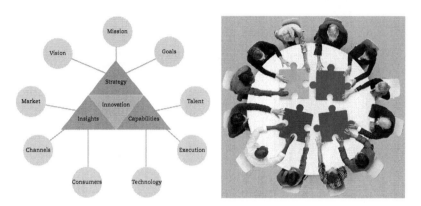

Teams and networks

Much has been written about the challenges of management, but today the main concern that needs to be addressed is how to manage organizations to attain high performance and quality standards given unprecedented speed of change, the increasing number of people and parties involved, and uncertain production chains that require quick fixes and effective synchronization.

Organizations are increasingly complex and operations involve interactions between people who work in different divisions and form inter-disciplinary, multi-gender, and multi-generation combinations, with different levels of responsibility and leadership. Yet all share the same pressing challenge to achieve optimal cooperation to attain synergy utilizing their talent, abilities, and capacity to achieve common goals.

To manage today's challenges it is important to understand the causes and effects of disturbances, and develop the best instruments to avoid wastage of time and efforts. Among them, agility provides the necessary flexibility to find solutions and resolves unexpected situations.

In today's highly competitive environment the focus on performance commonly overshadows the ability to change. Organizations cannot attain performance excellence unless they embrace change.

In another book, organizational effectiveness experts Edward Lawler and Christopher Worley show how organizations can be "built to change" to become sustainable and succeed in today's global economy. *Built to Change* (2006) is focused on practices and designs that organizations can adopt to facilitate change. The authors emphasize that organizations that foster continuous change have the following characteristics:[10]

- Are closely connected with their environment
- Reward employees for experimentation
- Learn continuously about new practices and technologies
- Are committed to continuously improving performance
- Pursue strategies of competitive advantages

Some agile notes on agility

Here is a summary of agile suggestions for "agilizing" agility in the organization.

- Organizational performance is a holistic framework. Hence the most effective approach to attaining agility is to take a holistic approach that reaches across the organization

10   http://www.edwardlawler.com/builttochange.html

- Building organizational agility requires focused leadership and management in organizational strategies and planning

- While strategies create a vision for agility, how to start and what steps are necessary to get there involves planning favorable and agile conditions across the organization

- Capabilities congruent with the organization's mission and vision to make agility sustainable in the long run must be developed

But any models, frameworks, structures, or strategies are merely guidelines an organization can *adopt* and *adapt* when they satisfy needs and expectations. Management is a science, yes, but the people who actually deploy management in organizations, in addition to management knowledge they have, need to have creativity and artistic acumen to develop an agile masterpiece.

Carrying out such management work makes organizations unique based on the talents, abilities, and commitment of people, and the capabilities of leaders. There are common denominators to selecting the best management model: agility aims to deploy strategies that lead to continuous improvement by people who are happy where they work and eager to optimize personal with organizational objectives.

Some words of caution:

- Agility networks need to be aware that, inevitably, there are people who are obstacles to change and organizational barriers, such as existing norms, rules, structures, and processes that slow things down

- Managers who have not participated in self-organized networks may introduce constraints, often in unintentional ways

- Lack of genuine customer engagement leaves work teams and agile networks pushed into tactical issues instead of innovative solutions

- Unavoidable political forces often press an us-versus-them mentality that accompanies any potentially successful impetus for change

- Problems are exacerbated when managers try to make teams work "harder": this ends in burnouts, losing focus and thereby obstructing improvement

To make an organization agile requires committed leaders and acceptance from the people who work *in* and *for* the organization that agility, innovation, continuous improvement, high performance, and quality standards are integral elements of the organizational mission.

Part III

Human-Centered Management and Sustainable Quality (SQ)

8

SQ foundations model

Human-Centered Management and SQ

Compared with other efficiency-driven innovation methods, the uniqueness of this model is embedded in these attributes:

- Integration of the three most important people-centered management areas: customers, employees, leadership

- Articulation of economic foundations of demand (customers/community/market) and supply (employees/producers) with managerial principles and practices

- 21st-century innovation vested in management theories identified among the most influential of the 20th century by the Academy of Management

- Comprehensive solution for organizations seeking high performance in the global challenges of the VUCA (volatile, uncertain, complex, ambiguous) environment

Part II discussed four of the five pillars of the Human-Centered Management model for organizations in the global VUCA environment of the 21st century: 1) human capital, 2) disruption resilience, 3) talent management, and 4) agility. These four pillars are now integrated and synchronized with the fifth pillar, the Sustainable Quality (SQ) model of performance assessment. This is the component necessary to allow organizations to monitor improvement and identify levels of performance, and the difference between performance and sustainable quality standards.

The five pillars reinforce each other to support the structure and organizational strategies to deal with disruptions and competitive forces in the "knowledge economy and society". The five pillars interact to improve organization productivity and competitiveness to face the challenges of the Fourth Industrial Revolution identified by Klaus Schwab, the founder of the World Economic Forum, at WEF's 2016 meeting.

Pillars 1, 2, 3, and 4 of the HCM model provide the basic foundations for organizations to advance in the 21st century and pillar 5 builds in the systematic assessment mechanism necessary to strengthen internal consistency, high performance, and the quality standards to project excellence to customers, markets, and communities.

What is *not* quality in the 21st century?

The Merriam-Webster dictionary defines quality as a characteristic or feature of something.

Wikipedia includes a number of definitions for quality. Among them, quality in business refers to the superiority of something. In philosophy, quality is an attribute of something. In physics, a property of something. All these quality definitions are only qualifying adjectives of an object and do not reflect, represent, or are associated with *sustainable quality, or the quality standards of the 21st century.* In other words, quality is not guaranteed by posting a quality banner on a product. And today well-informed customers are no longer misled by banners or words, but need proof of excellence to secure quality standards and a constant demand. Consequently organizations must demonstrate quality standards built on high performance and continuous improvement of products and services to secure a competitive edge in the industry.

What is quality, as in SQ?

In the 21st century quality is embedded in people and organizational efforts to produce and deliver excellence to meet needs and expectations of customers, and in sync, satisfy the needs and expectations of employees and all stakeholders in socially responsible organizations.

Producers and consumers: beware of real and fake quality!

Part III presents the management foundations necessary to recognize the difference between performance and the quality standards embedded in SQ. To start the discussion it is necessary to clarify that although performance can be high or low, *quality* is present or not in a product or service, therefore to say high quality or low quality in reality means uttering the qualifying adjective dimension described above and demonstrates ignorance of the fundamentals of 21st-century quality standards. From the management point of view this is critical because the prestige associated with quality standards in organizations in all sectors and worldwide has generated widespread misleading assumptions and abuses of the quality trademark. Unscrupulous parodies and distortions have harmed the quality paradigm and forced changes to highlight the differences, to such an extent that leading quality programs like National Quality Awards have changed the term "quality" to "excellence". The United States original Baldrige National Quality Award is now called the Baldrige Performance Excellence Program and the EFQM, which stands for European Foundation of Quality Management, is now called the EFQM Excellence Model.[1] Devious quality tactics affects all of us working in the improvement of sciences and quality management, as much as customers and producers at large. But like everything else, here there are also costs and benefits. On the supply side, counterfeit quality has brought much attention to advance the study of quality management in organizations. On the demand side, customers have learned to pay more attention to quality beyond quality banners or operators in call centers stating that *a phone call will be recorded for quality purposes*. Needless to say although some of these claims may be legitimate given the growing number of organizations deploying SQ that must collect customers' feedback to drive improvement; not all quality claims are genuine.

SQ fundamental principles

In the global VUCA environment, the wellbeing of people is one of the central factors to attain **ESTE BSD (Balanced Sustainable Development)** (economic, social, technological, environmental). Figure 8.1 shows the central role of people in the ESTE BSD model.

---

1   Baldrige Performance Excellence Program http://www.nist.gov/baldrige/; EFQM http://www.efqm.org/the-efqm-excellence-model

FIGURE 8.1   ESTE Balanced Sustainable Development
Source: author

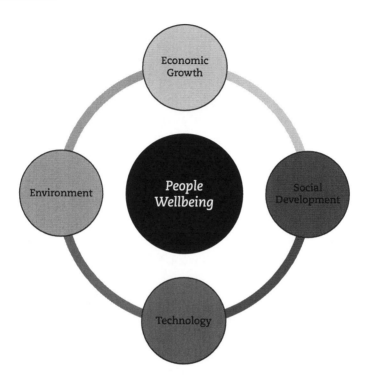

Characteristics of ESTE BSD

- People are responsible for organizations' sustainability to foster economic growth leading to inclusive societies worldwide.

- Since organizations are the basic unit of economic progress and customers the reason for organizations to exist, then SQ organizations are critical to foster growth and development.

- Organizations cannot be improved unless people improve themselves first. Here education plays a crucial role in sustainability.

SQ and organizational development

- Organizations exist because there are customers who demand their products/services.

- Well-informed customers/users demand products and services with quality standards.

- In VUCA environments, organizations' sustainability depends on continuous improvement and quality standards.

- In the age of the internet and open access to information, easy comparisons of products and services drives the competitive capacity based on quality standards essential for survival and sustainability.

- Organizations cannot meet the needs, expectations, and demands of "external customers" unless they meet first the needs of employees and all the people who work *in* and *for*[2] the organization. Although this seems to be common sense, it is less common than it should be.

- The four pillars discussed previously, human capital, disruption resilience, talent management, and agility, need to pass the SQ test to attain organization sustainability. The relationships between the four pillars and the fifth SQ pillar are shown in Figure 8.2.

---

2   The difference between *in* and *for* is important. Although all people work *in* an organizations, to work *for* the organization implies unequivocal commitment to foster the organizational goals and targets, sharing values and ethics.

FIGURE 8.2   Quality management is central to an organization's sustainability

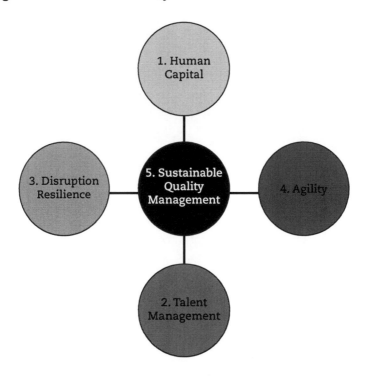

Getting ready to deploy SQ

- SQ is not an isolated issue; it is a concern for the whole organization

- The **external client** is most important

- The satisfaction of needs and expectations of external clients guides management and production

- The **internal clients** (employees and stakeholders) are essential to produce and deliver quality products and services to external clients/users
- Collaboration in teamwork and networks are important elements for continuous improvement and quality standards
- Effective communication between people increases performance and productivity and minimizes conflict
- Facts and data collection are important; gossip and guessing are not
- Main concern is to find solutions, *not problems*
- Long-term achievement prevails over short-term gain
- SQ is a model centered on people as a necessary condition to increase the rate of return on capital investment in education and training[3]

On the road to SQ standards

- Constructive Leadership is an organizational imperative at all levels of supervision
- The more people in the organization understand the benefits of SQ (and the costs of low performance), the better the results
- Full support for SQ teams and agile networks is needed to expedite continuous performance improvement across the organization

---

3   Beer *et al.* (2016) report that in 2015 employee training and education expenditures reached US$160 billion in the United States and US$356 billion globally with a low return on investment, because learning does not lead to better organization performance when people revert to old ways of doing things.

- Spread the SQ initiative to every division of the organization
- SQ is contagious; news of organizational quality spreads rapidly to external communities
- Focus organizational mission and vision on satisfaction of consumers' needs and expectations
- Strengthen organizational climate with happy employees oriented to customers
- Stimulate creativity, innovation, and risk-taking aimed at improvement (no risk, no gain)
- Reward personal responsibility for innovation and agility
- Allow experimentation and take failure as a necessary step in continuous improvement
- Monitor and reward SQ achievements
- Permanently evaluate results to systematize continuous improvement and SQ as organizational standards

Benefits of SQ

- Higher customer retention rate
- Fewer complaints from customers
- Reduction of costs
- Higher revenues
- Increased job satisfaction
- Improved organizational climate
- Highly productive labor relations
- Low labor turnover

- Higher returns on investment
- Increased productivity
- Increased competitiveness
- Improved organization image
- Increased prestige in markets and the community
- Maximum use of available resources

Costs of low performance

- Clients' complaints
- The need to re-do processes
- Work duplication
- Misuse of time
- Labor conflicts
- High absenteeism
- High turnover
- Volatile organizational climate
- Low trust
- Loss of resources
- Loss of clients
- Loss of revenues

9

The fifth pillar: Sustainable Quality (SQ)

SQ, the fifth pillar of the HCM model, is built on an organizational framework including instruments to measure performance in a systematic way to attain continuous improvement across the organization to meet SQ requirements. The SQ model allows the organization to evaluate internal performance and can objectively compare productivity and competitive standards with quality deploying peers.

The SQ model is normative, not prescriptive [1] implying that organizations are free to select people responsible for specific outcomes and results based on talent, creativity, and acumen (rather than organizational charts) who choose the variables, processes, programs, and proposals that can most effectively drive the organization to continuous improvement and SQ standards. Chapter 11 presents guidelines to develop the Organization Improvement Report aimed to conduct systematic organizational assessment of performance and improvement.

---

1   Where normative means using systematic guidelines and prescriptive means unbending, regulatory, dogmatic, or inflexible.

The SQ model consists of 7 Management Areas and 35 Assessment Elements. Management Areas 1, 2, and 3 are people based, representing HCM focus. This is aligned with higher point scores in Management Areas 1, 2, and 3 (190, 180, and 170, respectively). Management Areas 4, 5, 6, and 7 are process-centered areas designed to support organization development and sustainability. MA 4, Structure and Strategy, draws a maximum of 160 points to show the importance of organizational planning. The other three MAs, MA 5 Technology and Knowledge Management, MA 6 Support Processes, and MA 7 Vertical and Horizontal Integration and Environment Care, each draw 100 points.

Figure 9.1 shows the central role of customers/users and the interactions with the other six Management Areas. The customer focus characterizes all quality management and assessment methodologies.

FIGURE 9.1   **Seven Management Areas and scores**

TABLE 9.1   Human-Centered Management for Quality Sustainability

Management Area	Max. Score Area	Assessment Elements	Max, Element Score
1. Customers' satisfaction Markets Society	190	1.1 - Customers' satisfaction 1.2 - Market knowledge 1.3 - Community Improvement commitment 1.4 - Assessment system and instruments used 1.5 - Results report	1.1 - 50 1.2 - 35 1.3 - 35 1.4 - 20 1.5 - 50
2. Employees' wellbeing Stakeholders	180	2.1 - Employees' needs satisfaction and organization climate 2.2 - Performance measurement & merit recognition 2.3 - Training Human Capital. Talent Management development 2.4 - Assessment system and instruments used 2.5 - Results report	2.1 - 40 2.2 - 35 2.3 - 35 2.4 - 20 2.5 - 50
3. Constructive Leadership	170	3.1 - Constructive leadership for quality 3.2 - Resilience leadership & quality teams 3.3 - Agile leadership & quality networks 3.4 - Assessment system and instruments used 3.5 - Results report	3.1 - 40 3.2 - 30 3.3 - 30 3.4 - 20 3.5 - 50
4. Structure & Strategies	160	4.1 - Organization Mission and Vision for sustainability 4.2 - Organization resilient structure 4.3 - Organization agile strategies 4.4 - Assessment system and instruments used 4.5 - Results report	4.1 - 40 4.2 - 30 4.3 - 30 4.4 - 20 4.5 - 40

Category	Max	Items	Score
5. Technology. Knowledge Management	100	5.1 - Technology	20
		5.2 - Data management and analytics	20
		5.3 - From information to knowledge management for quality and sustainability	20
		5.4 - Assessment system and instruments used	10
		5.5 - Results report	30
6. Quality in Support Processes	100	6.1 - Economics & financial management	30
		6.2 - People management (hiring, promotion, firing methods)	15
		6.3 - Infrastructure management & maintenance	15
		6.4 - Assessment system and instruments used	10
		6.5 - Results report	30
7. Integration Benchmarking Environment care	100	7.1 - Vertical integration: Supply chain management	20
		7.2 - Horizontal Integration: Benchmarking and Constructive Competition	20
		7.3 - Environment care (internal and external)	20
		7.4 - Assessment system and instruments used	10
		7.5 - Results report	30
Max Score	1,000	Sustainable Quality & Excellence in Management	1,000

SQ framework and point scores

Table 9.1 shows the frame of the SQ Model identifying the 7 Management Areas and the 35 Assessment Elements including maximum scores for Assessment Elements and Management Areas.

The IPIEM SQ Cycle: Measuring improvement

Figure 9.2 and Tables 9.2 and 9.3 present the instrument used to measure improvement in five stages and scoring guidelines. Figure 9.2 shows the five stages of progress in the IPIEM SQ Cycle: 1) idea, 2) planning, 3) implementation, 4) evaluation, and 5) continuous improvement. Improvement in all the variables included in the 35 Assessment Elements are scored using this instrument.

FIGURE 9.2   IPIEM SQ Cycle

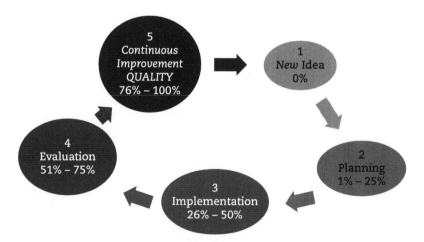

Discretion is advised to assess and report improvement in each one of the five stages observing whether the process is starting, progressing, or is mature and well developed. The differences between the five stages are clarified in Table 9.2. These percentages are applied to observed advances in the variables used in each Assessment Element to calculate partial and total SQ point scores.

TABLE 9.2   **Scoring improvement of Assessment Elements**

Progress Stages	Details	Relative percentage
1. New Idea	Idea exists. No further plan	0%. All people have good ideas to give to organizations. Only those ideas that advance to plans are valid.
2. Planning	A plan is advancing. No further implementation.	1 – 25%
3. Implementation	Plan has been implemented and aligned with other operations. No progress evaluation.	26 – 50%
4. Evaluation	Plan is fully integrated in operations and has reached systematic evaluation of progress.	50 – 75%
5. Continuous improvement	Plan completely deployed and integrated in operations. Assessment shows consistent evidence of continuous improvement.	76 – 100%

TABLE 9.3   **Understanding the difference between performance and SQ standards**

SQM Model requirements	Score	Standard
Maximum	800 – 1,000 points	Excellence – Sustainable Quality
Over	+600	Minimum for quality standard
Below	–600	Performance. NOT QUALITY

Quality for an elite and quality for all

National Quality Award programs (NQAs) worldwide provide support and improvement for the elite among organizations in all sectors. The objective of NQAs is to incentivize and guide organizations to pursue quality standards based on concrete evidence of continuous improvement of performance, productivity, and competitiveness by deploying the criteria of NQAs. The comprehensive HCMxSQ in general and the SQ assessment model in particular share values and requirements with National Quality Award programs worldwide, but instead of supporting an elite of organizations as do the NQAs, it opens access to organizations of all sizes, in all sectors, and in countries worldwide to similar standards but with the freedom to adjust to particular organizational goals and objectives and management rigor.

The Human-Centered Management SQ model embedded in Pillar 5 contrasts with other process-centered continuous improvement methods and techniques, such as Lean Management, Scoreboard, Scrum, and ISO norms, which share a deeper technical orientation, making them more difficult to deploy in organizations without the support of specialist consultants.

Leaders, employees, and stakeholder in organizations are free to *adopt* the five pillars of the HCM SQ model and *adapt* them to meet particular organizational needs with systematic assessment of improvement in the 7 Management Areas deployed and 35 Assessment Elements.

Testing reliability and validity of SQ standards

It is important to note a particular characteristic of the SQ model. The 7 Management Areas share two common Assessment Elements: Assessment System Instruments and Results (Table 9.1) These Assessment Elements indicate the importance of choosing reliable instruments to collect information necessary to validate the results. In contrast with other efficiency-seeking models, the SQ model also requires systematic assessment of the instruments used to assess performance and improvement. This is largely based on evidence that organizations tend to *adopt* instruments used in other environments and although this may be a convenient alternative, all instruments used in SQ must be tested and *adapted (improved)* to meet the specific needs of the organization. The use of unreliable, untested instruments has high potential to generate biased results, wasting time, efforts, and resources.

I often observe that people in organizations *adopt* instruments available (online or at hand) but fail to *adapt* them, obstructing improvement. It is fine to *adopt* instruments to avoid duplication of efforts but it is essential to test them to obtain valid results. I recommend using the creative minds of people in the organization to create reliable instruments to measure performance improvement.

7 Management Areas and 35 Assessment Elements

Management Area 1: Customer focus, markets, and communities/society (190 points)

If organizations don't have customers
They don't have reason to exist (author).

In market systems, the sustainability of organizations in the productive sector depends on customers. Thus a basic requirement for all organizations is to systematically collect information about customers' needs, preferences, and expectations to guide the design of products, services, and delivery methods. It is reported that organizations need to gain 10 new customers to compensate for the costs of one customer leaving.[1] In the knowledge economy, a thorough understanding of consumers can make the difference between success and downfall. Organizations benefit from collecting information from increasingly well-informed customers and using it to innovate. Consumers' information helps optimize production processes and management practices to meet their needs and keep customers' loyalty and engagement.

Customer focus

These are some of the questions organizations need to respond to in order to assess performance and report improvement and knowledge of variables in Assessment Element 1.1:

- Who are our customers?

- Where do they come from?

- What are their needs?[2]

- Why do they prefer our products/services over our competitors? (Benchmarking)

- Will customers' preferences change—or remain stable—in the near future and why?

1   Average commonly used in NQA programs in which I have served.
2   Review Maslow's Hierarchy of Human Needs in Part I.

- How effective and efficient is the organization's customer service division at providing fast solutions?

- Is the organization agile to ensure the best customer solution with least possible effort and cost?

- How can organizations benefit from using customers' talent?

- Given the abundance of information that customers have available to compare and select preferences, is the organization optimizing customers' talent to improve products and services and anticipate the design of new products?

Instruments to measure customer satisfaction/expectations
Verbal/meetings:

- Train all personnel to inquire and collect information about visitors and customers' level of satisfaction

- Have a customer service office

- Conduct focus groups

Printed surveys/questionnaires:

- Use of brief exit questionnaires

- Suggestion boxes

Digital approaches

- Customers' questionnaires (short, concise, easy, never exceed one page with brief but relevant questions)
    - Closed questions
    - Open questions

- Customer surveys (multiple choice)

- Websites, blogs

- Support via phone and email

A personal survey to assess customers' responsibility for SQ

1. Do you assume your quality responsibility as a **customer**?

2. Do you provide **constructive complaints** when you get a product or service which does not meet your needs or expectations? Do you complain, **not only for your own benefit, but to benefit other customers who will come after you?**

3. When you buy a product or service that does not satisfy your needs and expectations, **do you take time and make the effort to inform** the person and organization where you bought it or received it?

4. How do you make sure the organization **has not ignored your complaint,** but the representative is aware and acknowledges that in reality you are helping the organization improve the product or service?

5. What is your level of **effectiveness in providing constructive complaints?**

Market focus

These are questions organizations need to answer in Assessment Element 1.2:

- What are the market segments where customers come from?

- What drives their preferences? (tastes, prices, needs)

- What are the characteristics of customers' cohorts?

- Are there differences among customers' cohorts? If so, what?

- Which is the next market focus for the organization?

Community focus (organization social responsibility)

Customers come from communities (local, national, or global). Prosperous communities help organizations grow. Precarious communities can induce organizations to fail.

- What are some concrete actions and strategies the organization conducts to improve the community?

- How does the organization manage its social responsibility?

The following assessment methods and instruments serve as guides for the organizations on selecting appropriate items to conduct and record performance and continuous improvement in contingent elements of Management Area 1.

Assessment methods and instruments

In the organization improvement report (OIR), the organization describes the system used in data collection and analysis, and the instruments used to assess performance improvement and identify areas of improvement in this Management Area.

Results

Show results obtained in the variables, processes, programs, plans, etc. included in the Assessment Elements of this Management Area.

Management Area 2: Employees and stakeholders (180 points)

Increasing importance of talent management

Companies and countries will increasingly compete for the best and the brightest. Talent is driving economic growth anchored in a globally mobile creative class encompassing five generations of workers. Today the competition for talent comes not only from another company down the street, but also from employers on the other side of the world. It will be a seller's market with talented individuals having many choices. And countries and companies will need to brand themselves as locations of choice to attract this pool of talent (World Economic Forum, 2011, p. 7).

Employees' satisfaction and organizational climate

HCM SQ identifies all the people who work *in* and *for* the organizations (employees and stakeholders) as the producers of products and services and as internal clients. This particular identity emphasizes that internal clients are able to satisfy the needs and expectations of external clients and quality standards only after the organization can satisfy their needs and expectations.

Although the principal mission of the organization is satisfaction of external customers, organizations cannot produce and offer quality standards unless internal clients are satisfied to work with quality standards.

To supervise performance and assess improvement in the variables included in the 5 Assessment Elements of Management Area 2, it is imperative to read and understand the implications of the chapters on: 1) Disruption innovation, 2) Human capital, 3) Talent management, and 4) Agility because all impact employees.

It is critical to recall that, in the 21st century, the importance of human capital and talent management has surpassed the importance of capital (money) in organizations. Therefore the amount of human capital that every person who works in the organization possesses strengthens the organization when synchronized with effective talent management aiming to optimize organizational results.

Workforce demands are changing constantly, so resilience and agility to align employees with dynamic forces is necessary to move forward. In rapidly changing environments individual responsibility—instead of dependency and control—becomes essential to optimize collaboration, cooperation, decision-making, and problem-solving. SQ–high performance organizations promote collaboration and reward employees for individual accomplishments to stimulate resilient long-term teams responsible for long-range projects, programs, and plans in high synchronicity with short-term agile networks integrated by creative risk-takers and volunteer members responsible for innovation across the organization.

Diversity across the organization is important to deploy effective strategies to innovate, deal successfully with disruptions, adopt change, and advance in the talent economy.

Creativity-supporting elements in work environments

Studies on creative environments and ergonomics conducted by Jan Dul and associates (Dul *et al.*, 2012; Dul and Ceylan, 2014) add new insight to a long list of research literature on employees' satisfaction discussed in previous chapters. These studies confirm that creativity-supporting environments improve employee performance and product innovation based on information gathered in the Creativity Development Quick Scan. This instrument is an objective creativity assessment of employees' preferences that includes 21 factors, 9 social-organizational and 12 physical work environment characteristics, which enhance creativity in the organizational climate. Table 10.1 shows 21 factors in order of employees' preference according to these studies conducted in 2012 and based on 2,400 observations in 100 companies.

TABLE 10.1   **Twenty-one creative supporting elements in the work environment**

Element ranking	Elements
1	Challenging job
2	Autonomy in job
3	Teamwork
4	Quantity of light
5	Daytime
6	Any window view
7	Coaching supervisor
8	Recognition of creative ideas

→

Element ranking	Elements
9	Time for thinking
10	Indoor climate (physical)
11	Creative goals
12	Furniture
13	Task rotation
14	Incentives for creative results
15	Sound
16	Window view to nature
17	Privacy
18	Smell
19	Calming colors
20	Indoor plants/flowers
21	Inspiring colors

The following are basic questions that quality-seeking organizations need to answer to assess and manage satisfaction of the needs and expectations of employees.

- Who are the people who work in our organization?

- Where do they come from?

- What are their main needs?[3]

- Why do they prefer to work in this organization instead of in competitive organizations? (Benchmarking)

- How systematic is the organization to evaluate employees' needs and provide agile and effective solutions?

- Are employees agile in responding to the demands of the organization?

- How is diversity assessed and improved in the organization?

3   Review Maslow's Hierarchy of Human Needs in Part I.

- Who are the stakeholders (owners, investors, executives, managers)?

- Why did they take the risk and invest in the organization?

- What do investors expect in return? Consider investments in employees' development and returns to capital investment.

- How can the organization demonstrate that employees and stakeholders are "sailing in the same boat" and are collectively and jointly responsible to share the benefits of success as much as the costs of failure?

Performance measurement and merit recognition

Mutual trust and commitment are critical items in organizations, but trust and commitment are not easy to evaluate.

- What does the organization do to create a trustful work environment aimed at improving individual performance and organizational productivity?

- How does the organization recognize and compensate employees' commitment to the organization?

- How does the organization assess employees' attitudes, knowledge, and skills that optimize job satisfaction?

- How does the organization recognize employees' creativity, agility, and innovations in rapidly changing and uncertain environments?

- How does the organization ensure diversity in terms of gender and age of employees, and ensure that the workforce has an international background?

- How does the organization reward the achievements and merits of employees?

- Given common and continuous disruptions in the work-place, how does the organization provide flexibility and a "freedom to fail to meet the target next time" method?

- How does the organization offer employees opportunities to work and focus on agile projects (rather than fixed positions) to better reflect agility trends in the industry?

- How does the organization plan for long-term structural work teams and short-term strategic agile networks aimed to foster innovation?

- How does the organization assess resilience and innovation in employees and across divisions?

- How does the organization assess effectiveness of internal relations between employees?

- How does the organization assess employees' relationships with external customers and the community?

Talent management: Training and development

In the talent economy and increasingly in the open global talent economy, human capital accumulation is the prevailing trend (Barry *et al.*, 2013). In this environment organizations have unprecedented opportunities to partake in the talent revolution; otherwise the cost of shying away and undervaluing the impact of human talent will make it increasingly difficult to manage unavoidable disruptions that affect organizations worldwide.

Talent management assessment:

- Demonstrate the organization's strength in having leadership that understands the benefits of and provides effective talent management

- Does the organization have talent management programs under supervision of the executive level supported by supervisors from the *people management office?* [4]

- How does the organization distinguish people's talent necessary in structural (long-term) work teams from talent required by strategic (short-term) agile network members responsible for innovating products, optimizing budgets, and maximizing results?

- How does the organization measure and rewards employees' creativity, resilience, agility, and innovation drive?

Assessment methods and instruments

Again, in the OIR, describe the system used in data collection and analysis and the instruments used to assess performance improvement.

Results

Show results obtained in the variables, processes, programs, plans, etc. included in the Assessment Elements of this Management Area.

---

4   Studies demonstrate that in the knowledge economy talent management strategies are so important to improve performance and attain SQ that TM must be an organizational goal, instead of a program exclusively supervised by the people management office. As has been stated, Human-Centered Management substitutes people management for human resource management based on a fundamental principle that people are not another organization resource, but the reason for organizations to exist.

Need for leadership innovation

> Give me a fish and I will eat for a day.
> Give me seven fish and I will live for a week.
> Teach me to fish and I will survive.
> (Chinese proverb)

This centuries-old Chinese proverb fits closely with the fundamental principles of Constructive Leadership (CL) as the organizational engine of SQ management model. CL is built in the constructive capacity leaders need to motivate and meet the needs of the employees they lead. CL highlights abilities to help others become self-reliant and independent to accomplish deeds and in turn become examples for others.

The CL analysis presented in Management Area 3 is more extensive than other Areas because it is a new leadership approach designed for SQ-driven organizations that has significant impact on the wellbeing of employees to achieve the purpose that they work *in* as much as *for* the organization. In a preliminary discussion of the 2017 meeting of the World Economic Forum, Klaus Schwab emphasized the importance of *responsive and responsible leaders* to re-ignite global economic growth leading to inclusive societies.[5]

The following are principles and practices that underline CL embedded in the SQ model.

- CL is not exclusively related to top positions in the organization, but entails a way of thinking, acting, of giving and receiving, where all participate and everybody gains. It is an opportunity and responsibility for mentoring and coaching, and a responsibility and opportunity for continuous learning from peers.

---

5   https://www.weforum.org/events/world-economic-forum-annual-meeting-2017

- Self-confidence is a fundamental condition in CL to lead, value, and respect other people. Self-reliance creates a virtuous cycle of personal wellbeing necessary to guide people in the organization to higher levels of performance, productivity, and competitiveness.

- CL is the engine that drives organizations to quality standards required for sustainability.

A clear understanding of the differences between traditional administrative stereotypes and CL facilitates organizational change. While bosses and administrators of the industrial past tend to show preference for hierarchical control to influence and convince[6] others, in contrast constructive leaders empower people, delegate decision-making, and motivate people to be accountable for continuous improvement and better results.

Table 10.2 clarifies the differences between sources of power and identifies sources that empower CL in the SQ model.

Evolution towards Constructive Leadership

Chapter 2 presents a comprehensive review of the origins of Human-Centered Management in the 20th century. HCM expanded to countries around the world largely anchored to a new style of people-centered leadership that contrasts deeply with process-resource-centered management methods that characterized hierarchical/bureaucratic organizational administrations. A classic example used to show the leadership shift was associated with the auto industry in Japan. In the 1970s, Kiichiro Toyoda, the founder of Toyota auto manufacturer and a follower of Edwards Deming's

---

6   "Convincing" is a commonly misunderstood and misleading concept. In reality nobody can convince another person, but the other person convinces her/himself, realizing tangible benefits of the proposed transaction.

Total Quality Management movement (Chapter 2), changed the way cars were designed and produced, shifting from a supply-side vision to a demand-driven/consumer focus. On the production side Toyoda identified that leadership for continuous improvement and quality required: "helping people to understand what management expects in a friendly atmosphere and where everybody works happily and is responsible for results". Developing work environments that contribute to make employees happy became a precondition for increased performance and productivity necessary to satisfy a large diversity of customers and growing demands.

TABLE 10.2 **Hierarchy of power**

Sources of Power	Features
I. Coercive power Source: coercion	Command over others based on controlling information or imposing difficulties
II. Enticement power Source: monetary or material compensation	Command over others based on compensation for special favor
III. Position power Source: position in organization	Based on the responsibility attached to a position
IV. Expert power Source: knowledge, experience	Granted by personal capacity and knowledge
V. Genuine power Source: emotional intelligence Constructive Leadership	Evolves from trust, empathy, understanding and capacity to create synergy with other people

Source: Lepeley (2001)

To distinguish focal differences between CL consistent with deployment of quality standards and traditional supervision in hierarchical organizations Table 10.3 contrasts characteristics of constructive leaders and bosses.

TABLE 10.3   Differences between constructive leaders and bosses

Constructive leaders	Bosses
Focus on people	Focus on processes
Inspire trust	Use control
Aim at long-term benefits	Follow short-term goals
Focus on finding solutions	Focus on finding problems
Incentive innovation	Perpetuate status quo
Promote change for continuous improvement	Favor repetitive activities
Foster freedom and responsibility for achievement	Follow rules and fear of change
Take failure as stages for improvement	Intolerant of failure and experimentation
Promote constructive competition[7]	Support destructive competition[8]
Effective negotiation	Command and control
Emphasis on Soft Skills[9]	Emphasis on technocracy

Source: Lepeley (2001)

To be able to recognize leadership style is important because it determines the organization's structure and strategies, the resilience capacity and agility, human capital growth, talent management, and the attainment of quality standards leading to sustainability. Confronted with the challenges of the global VUCA environment, organizations are pressed to change hierarchical structures to more functional matrix organizational designs where people share responsibility and accountability for performance and results to respond to rapidly evolving customer demands.

7   Constructive competition: win–win competition.
8   Destructive competition: One winner takes all.
9   Soft skills: people skills, effective communications, respect for diversity.

Effective change in work environments require constructive capacity and an increasingly agile leadership style to help organizations absorb, adapt, and adopt transformation ensuring that the benefits of change surpassed the costs of the status quo. Agility is essential for innovation. And innovation is embedded in risk-taking, trial and error, and unlearning obsolete schemes to learn new themes (Bonchek, 2016; Sandlin, 2017; Kenyon, 2017; Lepeley, submitted); all these are significant challenges for management and leadership. In global VUCA environments, Constructive Leadership values "failure" as a necessary risk to move forward that must be encouraged to innovate and attain sustainability (Birkinshaw and Haas, 2016).

The value of failure as learning process

In the 21st century many leaders and a high proportion of organizations are struggling with growth issues largely based on fear of failure. Although a growing number of senior executives acknowledge that failure is necessary to innovate and advance, and recognize potential benefits, still old structures and fears are deeply ingrained. Moreover when management is built on predictable patterns of efficiency, this drives supervisors to appear always in control of operations and unable to assume risk, obstructing potential innovation.

Birkinshaw and Haas (2016) present a proposal to resolve the failure conundrum supported by a decade of research on leaders and organization dynamics across industries. Their proposal is built on three steps.

1. Awareness of the benefits of failure

Train people to reflect on projects or initiatives that have failed. Acknowledge that this is not an easy task because reviewing past problems is an inherently painful effort and people prefer to invest time looking forward, not backward.

To help people learn from failure, guide them to ask the right questions and make them summarize all the benefits of the failed experience as well as the costs. Overall convey to people that when something does not advance as planned, the experience may still offer opportunities to challenge previous beliefs and provide valuable information to make adjustments for improvement. Make sure that the persons involved gain a positive experience and learn to address the following challenges: customers and market dynamics; organizational structure and strategy, workplace culture, and ongoing processes; learn new things about themselves and about other people in their teams; and gain incentives to choose better approaches in the future based on this experience.

2. Share lessons learned for collective benefit

From the organization dimension, the payoff of this failure analysis is to share learning experience with people across the organization and provide new ways to do old things, sharing information in forums, messaging, or blogs aimed to create a "constructive cycle of responsible failing". When information, ideas, and opportunities for improvement gained from unsuccessful projects are passed on and shared with others, the benefits of failure are magnified, increasing likelihood of success in the future. Birkinshaw and Haas emphasize that "The biggest mistake a leader can make is to shoot the messenger and bury the bad news". Reflecting on the positive side of failure allows people to gain trust in each other, increasing organizational goodwill, and contributes to build resilience on a clearer pathway to take action on risk and innovative ideas. Birkinshaw and Haas provide useful advice stating that learning from failure reviews work best when they are *fast*, *frequent*, and are *forward-looking* (FFF), and have unequivocal focus on learning and improvement.

3. Assess if FFF failure reviews help or hurt the organization

To consolidate a culture of positive failure implies conducting periodic evaluations to ensure that failure reviews are working and helping to improve employees' knowledge and advance organizational efficiency. This assessment is necessary to determine whether the failure rate is too high, too low, or just right. An increasing number of organizations are creating recognition and special awards to celebrate leanings from failure as an instrument to transform human failures into organization fortunes.

Organizations worldwide are seeking risk-taking abilities in employees and new hires as a valuable Soft Skill required to promote innovation necessary to gain competitive advantages (Lepeley and Albornoz, 2013).

Birkinshaw and Hall (2016) report the beneficial side of failure, citing the cases of two highly agile companies. 3M's chairman William McKnight says "The best and hardest work is done in the spirit of adventure and challenge … where … mistakes will be made". And Pixar's president, Ed Catmull stating: "Mistakes aren't a necessary evil. They aren't evil at all. They are an inevitable consequence of doing something new … and should be seen as valuable."

Birkinshaw and Hall (2016) developed a Project Review Worksheet to assess and keep record of risk-taking and learning that can help organization and division leaders to guide this process.[10]

10   https://hbr.org/resources/pdfs/hbr-articles/2016/04/Worksheet-Project-Review.pdf

Management Area 3: Constructive Leadership (170 points)

These are some of the questions to answer to assess advances, improvement, and consolidation of CL in organizations.

- How does the organization measure Constructive Leadership capacity among executive/senior leaders to secure a work environment for continuous improvement?

- How does the organization assess and ensure that executive/senior leaders communicate with and engage all employees?

    ○ How do leaders encourage frank, reciprocal communication throughout the organization?

    ○ How do leaders communicate key decisions and ensure these are understood by all employees involved?

- How does the organization measure and ensure that leaders are optimizing the talent of every person who works in the organization?

- How do leaders ensure that people work not only *in* but *for* the organization?

- How does the organization measure the Constructive Leadership ability and capacity of leaders of divisions, departments, projects, teams, and internal networks?

- How does the organization stimulate Constructive Leadership across the organization so that all employees know and deploy fundamental principles and practices linked to quality standards?

- How does the organization train new leaders in Constructive Leadership?

- How does the organization assess continuous improvement in social responsibility?

- How does the organization measure, promote, and ensure a continuous value-creation attitude among leaders to incentivize employees to adopt a similar attitude?

- How does the organization measure, promote, and ensure the win–win negotiation capacity of leaders across and outside of the organization?

- How do leaders in the organization build Constructive Leadership aimed to balance the organization's purpose and identity with creativity and innovation?

Leadership and resilience in **quality teams**

- At the highest executive level of the organization, who is responsible for resilience and organizing long-term quality teams?
  - How is this leadership responsibility measured?

- How does the organization select members and talent to organize long-term quality teams to direct and supervise continuous improvement?

- How does the organization measure relevance and secure continuous quality improvement in the organization's structure?

- How does the organization organize and evaluate the performance of quality team leaders in structural divisions, departments, units (responsible for principal processes of the organization)?

- How does the organization measure and assure effective communications throughout?

Leadership and agility in **quality networks** for sustainable quality

- At the highest executive level of the organization, who is responsible for agility and organizing short-term innovation networks?
  - How is this leadership responsibility measured?

- How does the organization select the talent pool and solicit volunteers to participate in short-term innovation networks responsible for the organization's agility?

- How does the organization measure *responsible failures* aimed toward innovation counting benefits of trials as unavoidable stages to advance, improve, and become sustainable?

- How does the organization measure the necessity and relevance of the organization's strategies to advance to continuous improvement, quality standards, and sustainability?

- How does the organization organize and evaluate the performance of innovation networks that support projects in divisions, departments, units?

- How does the organization measure and ensure talent diversity and harmony/effectiveness in innovation networks?

- How does the organization measure and assure effective communications throughout?

Assessment methods and instruments

In the OIR, the organization describes the system used in data collection and analysis, and the instruments used to assess performance improvement and identify areas of improvement in this management area.

Results

Show results obtained in the variables, processes, programs, plans, etc. included in the Assessment Elements of this Management Area.

Management Area 4: Structure and strategies (160 points)

Organization's mission and vision

- Is there a description of the organization's operations and environment, identifying products/services and key relationships with customers, users, suppliers, markets, and society/community (local, national, global if it is the case)?

- What is the explicit quality standard mission statement of the organization?[11]

11   The organization's mission statement in quality-driven organizations is concise and identifies: 1) customers/users as the main reason for the organization's existence; 2) explicit commitment to continuous improvement and quality standards; 3) items produced and delivered with special care for the

o How does the organization measure the relevance of its mission?

• Is the mission statement posted in visible places for everybody (customers and employees) to see?

• What is the explicit quality standard vision statement of the organization expressing present and future commitment to sustainability?[12]

• What is the organization governance system?

o How is effectiveness measured?

• How does the organization secure a matrix governance structure supporting sustainable quality principles and practices across divisions, departments, units?

o How are effectiveness and resilience measured?

• What are the communication channels between governing boards, senior leaders, and division/department leaders, to attain continuous improvement and quality standards across the organization?

Organization's structure

• What is the organization's structure?

o How are effectiveness and improvement measured?

---

wellbeing of the people who work in the organization; 4) the organizations conveys clear and solid principles of integrity, ethics, and social responsibility.

12 The organization's vision briefly and clearly spells out objectives to attain continuous improvement/learning of the people who work *in* and *for* the organization to offer quality standards to customers and suppliers.

- What is and how does the organization manage human capital (HC)?
  - How does the organization measure and accumulate HC?
  - How does the organization develop internal HC and hire external HC?
- How does the organization use HC to build disruption resilience?
  - How is resilience measured?
- How is the organization's resilience measured?
  - How is resilience monitored for continuous improvement?
- What systematic procedures does the organization use to organize long-term functional work teams?
  - How does the organization measure the relevance and deployment of its vision?
- What are the organization's main physical assets (buildings, technology capacity, others)?
  - How are assets measured and continuously improved?

Organization's strategies

- What is the system the organization uses to develop strategies?
  - How is effectiveness and improvement measured?
- What is, and how does the organization manage, talent?
  - How does the organization develop and measure talent?
  - How does the organization develop internal talent?

- How does the organization use talent to build agility?

  ○ How are effectiveness and resilience measured?

- What systematic procedures does the organization use to organize short-term *agile networks* of volunteer employees to advance change and secure innovation?

- How is organization agility measured?

  ○ How is agility continuously improved?

Assessment methods and instruments

In the OIR, the organization describes the system used in data collection and analysis, and the instruments used to assess performance improvement and identify areas of improvement in this management area.

Results

Show results obtained in the variables, processes, programs, plans, etc. included in the Assessment Elements of this Management Area.

Management Area 5: Technology and knowledge management (100 points)

Management Area 5 is critical to monitor and assess continuous improvement and objectively demonstrate quality standards that lead to the organization's sustainability.

Area 5 is focused on the selection and deployment of the best technology to transform the information the organization collects into knowledge necessary to optimize decision-making and the organization's management.

Technology is changing the way people live, communicate, think, and work, and impacting upon production, operations, and delivery in organizations in all sectors. Technology has significant impact upon every Management Area in organizations and in this case it is necessary to focus on Pillar 3 (talent management) and Pillar 5 (agility) to optimize results in Management Area 5.

Management Area 5 links technology with data collection and analysis, and the capacity of people in the organization to transform data into knowledge to optimize decision-making, risk taking, and advance innovation leading to continuous improvement, SQ, and organization sustainability.

Technology

The optimal selection of an IT system that meets the specific needs of the organization is a critical decision. Inadequate IT choices hinder operations, data collection and analytics, data sourcing and storage, and can prevent integration with older IT capabilities.

Resolving IT issues takes time, and people in the organization should be encouraged to discover and report IT problems to the executive level to ensure that IT updates are prioritized, improving work performance, productivity, and cyber security, which is today a growing concern for organizations worldwide.

Another important challenge for organizations is to synchronize the IT system with management needs, because although data collection and analytics are essential to improve performance quality standards, and competitive advantage, IT effectiveness depends on the degree of IT support and the level of technology. A good IT question to ask people in the organization is: "What would be the optimal IT system that can help us improve our decision-making capacity to improve performance as individuals and as an organization?"

Technology affects people and organizations in direct and indirect ways:

- For the first time in history, up to five generations are working together in one organization with very different technical skills. While young employees—millennials, post-millennials, Generation Z—are comfortable with digitization, older employees may have more trouble dealing with the newest technologies.

- Cloud-based platforms are linking computers with other digital devices, so information is accessible from everywhere. This facilitates employees' mobility and the organization's agility. However, some employees are complaining that organizations are using connectivity as a device to enable non-stop working!

- IT allows organizations to expand use of the cloud to run personalized applications such as MOOCs (massive open online courses), SPOCs (small private online courses), instructional videos, learning games, e-coaching, virtual classrooms, online performance support, and online simulations that are changing the way organizations train and track employees.

- New approaches to learning allow employees to educate and develop themselves using user-friendly IT digital devices to share knowledge. This is fostering a new culture of collaborative learning and networking.

- The power of collective intelligence is becoming crucial in the digital-learning transformation, transforming the structure of organizations from hierarchical to matrix.

- In this IT environment, organizations are no longer the exclusive owners of information because employees can empower themselves with their own knowledge, or with knowledge shared across the organization. On the positive side, this outcome has the potential to decrease the training costs of employees and solve the perennial problem of who will be the trainer.

McKinsey's study "Raising your digital quotient" (Catlin *et al.*, 2015) helps identify IT systems that provide foundations for key organizational processes and activities. It also assesses digital challenges based on needs assessment and three considerations that help to build a digital culture that empowers decision-making.

Connectivity

Evaluate utility and cost/benefit of technologies such as apps, personalization, and social media that can help the organization establish strong connections with consumer and user demands. These connections can also guide organizations on new product development. Encouraging customers/users to visit online platforms, or use email and social media outlets for feedback, saves costs of customers' and users' surveys necessary to collect information to make decisions for improvement.

Process automation

Focus IT and automation efforts on well-defined processes and conduct tests for optimization. Successful processes start envisioning the future state for each process, disregarding current constraints. Once that future state is described then relevant constraints should be reconsidered and added to the cost/benefit formula.

Two-speed IT

Today's rapidly changing consumer expectations put increasing pressure on the organization's IT system, requiring continuous monitoring, testing, learning, failing, adapting, and improving. To alleviate this pressure consider integration of two levels of IT speeds. One with slower IT speed capability aimed at supporting traditional operations and the core IT infrastructure, prioritizing data management with built-in security to keep business services reliable and trustworthy. Another high-speed IT used to deliver rapid results to customers, built on modular and agile interface technology to move quickly and deploy micro-services through dynamic devices and a personalized website.

Data management and analytics

A major challenge for people and organizations is no longer information scarcity, but information over-abundance and the need to discriminate between reliable and unreliable sources of information. The volume of information grows rapidly, and opportunities for improvement accelerate in parallel with increasing concerns over cyber security. Such concerns press organizations to develop analytical capacity to alleviate the work required to transform an organization's data into knowledge fostering improvement.

In my experience in quality management and organizational certification, I observed that organizations collect large amounts of data, but don't use it properly to make decisions to solve problems in order to advance. I advise leaders to encourage employees to regularly look at old data with new eyes, aiming to strengthen agility to identify improvement opportunities.

Quality-driven organizations encourage creativity and agility and increasingly incorporate external data sources, ranging from local demographics to weather forecasts and social media to improve decision-making. Social media is an important source of information, offering terabytes of nontraditional and unstructured data, conversations, photos, video, and streams of data flowing from sensors and monitored processes that help to create the organization's knowledge.

Here are questions the organization needs to ask and answer to evaluate data management.

- How does the organization collect and analyze information?

- How does the organization manage data collection to secure accuracy, integrity, reliability, timeliness, security, and confidentiality?

- How does the organization confirm that data is helping to improve decision-making at all levels and is used by all responsible managers and employees?

- How does the organization ensure data management and operational support helps decision-makers improve results?

- Does the organization have systematic training programs on data management to help employees develop skills aimed at continuous improvement?

- How does the organization ensure agile data management strategies, essential to foster the organization's agility so that it is able to face rapid changes in environments and technology?

Transforming data into knowledge

In the 21st century exponential information growth puts **big data** and **analytics** at the top of organizational development. Data-driven strategies are transforming the way organizations make decisions, do business, and redesign core processes. Data-driven knowledge management is the new key for competitive advantage. With almost no exceptions, organizations collect volumes of information about principal and supporting processes, yet some organizations lack capacity to transform data into knowledge useful to optimize decisions.

Four decades ago Edwards Deming's total quality management pioneered systematic data collection and analysis to help organizations develop the capacity to monitor and assess performance in a systematic way.

More recently McKinsey mega-data management experts propose three mutually supportive capabilities to transform information into knowledge. First, the organization develops capacity to identify, combine, and manage multiple sources of data. Second, it develops capacity to build increasingly complex analytical models focusing on continuous improvement. Third, leaders improve their ability to make decisions and their capacity to transform the organization, using objective knowledge to improve decision-making (Barton and Court, 2013).

A clear vision of continuous improvement is essential to advance the quality transformation and cement the basis for SQ. Therefore leaders of organizations, supported by quality teams (long term) and agility networks (short-term innovative projects), need to invest time and energy aligning employees across the organization with the knowledge and technology necessary to improve outcomes and results.

A way of inspiring executives and employees to adopt agility that leads to continuous improvement (supported by technology) is to ask "What decisions can we improve if we have all the knowledge we need?"

As previously stated, when conducting technology assessment in the organization it is important to remember that technology is useful, but it is useless unless people can use it.

Assessment methods and instruments

In the OIR, the organization describes the system used in data collection and analysis, and the instruments used to assess performance improvement and identify areas of improvement in this Management Area.

Results

Show results obtained in the variables, processes, programs, plans, etc. included in the Assessment Elements of this Management Area.

Management Area 6: Support processes (100 points)

The SQ model is based on systematic evaluation of performance in the principal organizational processes, activities, and functions and the same continuous improvement requirements apply to all supporting processes. The supporting processes include economic and financial management, people management (originally called human resource management), maintenance of physical infrastructure and buildings, among others

Increasing organizational complexity is pressing for a growing number of supporting processes that require systematic assessment in Management Area 6.

Economics and financial processes

Economic efficiency and financial proficiency are essential elements in organization sustainability. Financial management is a key organizational concern to attain quality standards and requires constant monitoring of the following functions:

- Change in revenues
- Change in expenses
- Change in investment
- Change in investment returns

These are some questions organizations need to address in order to advance economic and financial sustainability:

- How does the organization ensure accounting system effectiveness is aligned with the organization operations and evolution?

- How does the organization demonstrate continuous improvement in financial management to support long-term sustainability?

- How agile is financial management to adjust to changes in the economy?

- Given the fundamental HCM SQ principle that organizations exist to serve customers who come from a community—and based on increasing research that organizations effectively involved with society have increasing rates of return on investment—how does the organization manage investments in systematic community improvement (Brown *et al.*, 2016)?

- How does the organization report investments in the community and society?

- What is the rate of return on investment in community improvement?

People management

The HCM SQ model is based on the principle that human beings are the reason for organizations to exist and are not merely another resource in organizations. This vision advances the paradigm shift proposed by HCM SQ identifying the division as **people management** (PM), as an update for the obsolescence of *humans as resources* and *human resource management*.

Human resources is a concept coined in the 20th century to match the imperatives of the industrial past, when employees were considered in parallel with other physical resources. This term is part of the status quo that overlooks how derogatory it may be toward employees. Nobody likes to be treated as a *resource*; nevertheless this is one among many concepts in management that needs update and innovation.

The conceptualization of humans as a resource collides with mounting evidence that in the knowledge economy, human capital and human talent determine progress to a higher degree than physical capital.

Human capital and effective talent management are increasingly needed to face disruptions. Consequently the people management division and its responsibilities in recruitment, training and development, compensation and benefits, employees' relations, work climate, safety, compliance, and firing policies are far more complex and pressing.[13]

One of the most important challenges for people management offices in the productive sector is the widespread lack of Soft Skills of employees and particularly among business graduates, applicants, and new hires, which organizations require to face the challenges of the global VUCA environment with increasing productivity and competitiveness (Lepeley and Albornoz, 2013; Massaro *et al.*,

---

13   Review Chapter 3 on the disturbances that affect organizations.

2016; Majluf, 2016). The change in organizational structure from hierarchical to matrix demands employees with greater independence in decision-making and more dependence to participate in teams organized to solve more complex problems that commonly require multidisciplinary approaches and better social attributes. The situation is reaching critical limits, inducing organizations to switch from traditional recruiting methods focused on school or college diplomas and course grades, to conducting interviews with applicants to observe their ability to communicate with others and their collaboration and problem-solving skills. Google has pioneered research on effective teams and innovative recruiting, leading the way with non-traditional strategies that are also useful for traditional companies worldwide.

Other PM innovation trends include the 2014 *Academy of Management Journal* article "Job titles as identity badges: How self-reflective titles can reduce emotional exhaustion" (Grant *et al.*, 2014). The article shows that outdated job titles have far-reaching implications for human capital and employees' identity; and employees who can create self-reflected job titles experience less emotional stress than employees in control groups. These results imply that self-reflected job titles can be an effective driver of identity expression and psychological security and reduce stress. Grant *et al.* (2014) emphasize the low costs associated with testing this strategy, which carries high potential to improve employees' wellbeing and organizational climate.

Grant *et al.* also highlight that job titles no longer generate the excitement or expectations they used to and an increasing number of organizations are using the creativity of employees to formulate their own job titles. For instance, Disney calls its theme park workers "Cast Members" and its engineers and multimedia experts "Imagineers." Subway's line workers are "Sandwich Artists."

Another company calls receptionists "Directors of First Impressions" while PR people are "Brand Evangelists" (Grant *et al.*, 2014).

For over a decade, London Business School Professor Dan Cable has viewed innovation in job titles as a legitimate tool for improving workers' attitudes. He states that traditional views of job titles are related to standardizations that send misleading signals and may even fail to attract the best applicants. Organizations need to recognize that job titles are powerful symbols of identity and must monitor their relevance among changing attitudes and outdated standards.

These are some of the questions that help identify the processes the people management department (PMD) needs to assess to monitor continuous improvement and innovation based on agile strategies:

- How does the organization ensure that PMD's policies align with the organization's mission, vision, and values in activities under its remit, and with continuous performance improvement?

- How does PMD ensure recruitment strategies that optimize continuous alignment with the organization's human capital and talent needs?

- How does PMD ensure optimal strategies which align the training of human capital and development of talent in the organization's workforce?

- How does PMD ensure fair and competitive compensation and benefits for all employees? How does the organization ensure the optimization of the work organizational climate?

- How does PMD ensure optimization of compliances and regulations with external agencies?

- How does PMD secure optimal diversity within its workforce (including a mixture of genders, ages, and nationalities) to meet the needs of the organization and match society's diversity?

- How does PMD develop and deploy firing policies that simultaneously meet the organization's values and needs, and the needs of departing employees?

- How does PMD manage emerging challenges and continuously support the development of *human capital* to strengthen *resilient, long-term work teams* across divisions in the organization?

- How does PMD support change and innovation based on talent identification and supporting leadership to help expedite agility in networks across divisions?

Physical infrastructure and maintenance

The same continuous improvement principles that apply to all organizational processes apply to buildings and infrastructure in quality-driven organizations. Some of the questions to assess these divisions include:

- How does the organization secure the wellbeing of the workforce in spaces and buildings that promote ergonomics and stimulate high productivity?

- How does the organization secure continuous improvement in the maintenance of buildings and infrastructure?

At this point it is useful to disclose a strategy I used when I was a senior examiner in National Quality Award programs and the leading person of examiners' teams visiting companies preselected to competing for the award. When we were carrying out the physical inspection of the facilities, I looked for a restroom far away from the executive offices. When I saw one I told my hosts (commonly top company executives) that I needed to make a visit to that restroom. I was immediately invited to go to the restrooms in the executive quarters, but I insisted I had to go to the closest restroom for employees because I discovered that this strategy invariably gave me outstanding information on how the company treated its people.

Assessment methods and instruments

In the OIR, the organization describes the system used in data collection and analysis, and the instruments used to assess performance improvement and identify areas of improvement in this Management Area.

Results

Show results obtained in the variables, processes, programs, plans, etc. included in the Assessment Elements of this Management Area.

Management Area 7: Integration, benchmarking, and environment care (100 points)

Vertical integration: Supply chain management

In the knowledge economy, organizations in all sectors recognize that effective vertical integration and supportive "supply chains" is increasingly complex and involves planning, information sharing to design value-added activities linking raw material to final products, and smart distribution logistics to deliver on time and meet customers' quality standards. Constant disruptions in markets and changes in customers' preferences press organizations to develop agile supply chain strategies to integrate multiple producers locally and globally. Organizations closely monitor disruptions in supply chains to manage risks and respond to sudden changes in economic, technological, and competitive environments to take advantage of emerging opportunities.

Quality-driven organizations invest to improve supply-chain capabilities, sharing quality principles and practices with suppliers and use it as an instrument to outperform competitors. In reality this business model is disrupting industries worldwide. Google, Amazon, Airbnb, and Uber are just a few examples of supply-chain agility innovators most visible in vertical integration.

In the global VUCA economy supply-chain operations are increasingly complex and harder to manage and disruptions are requiring increasing levels of trust and transparency to coordinate supply chains quickly, with agile performance expediting cross-functional decision-making to boost improvement, profitability, and sustainability.

Although supply chains vary widely between industries and organizations, successful performance depends to a large extent on the following factors:

- Human capital

- Constructive Leadership

- Talent management

- Logistics

- Capacity to differentiate new from outdated practices

- Innovation over standardized approaches

- Effective and efficient end-to-end data keeping and analysis

- Cross-functional decision-making

- Optimal IT support for applications and platforms that facilitate collaboration and analysis

- Continuous monitoring of customers and market metrics to ensure pursuit of quality standards and excellence as essential elements of competitive advantage

Vertical integration assessment:

- What is the organization's vertical integration strategy? How does it optimize customers' satisfaction and returns on investment in the supply chain?

- How does the organization ensure that the benefits of vertical integration and supply chains always surpass the costs of its supply chain?

- How does the organization secure continuous improvement of its vertical integration strategies by sharing quality principles and practices along the supply chain?

- What innovations in vertical integration have resulted in increasing competitive advantages for the organization?

- How agile is the vertical integration strategy of the organization in terms of its ability to expand production and sales, and compete in new regions?

Horizontal integration: Benchmarking and constructive competition

Benchmarking is a method initially used in land-surveying practices to compare ground elevations, which business has adopted and adapted to compare performance among organizations in the same industry.

Benchmarking, or comparing organization performance with peers, is an important practice in quality-driven organizations to confirm progress and achievements that the organization can celebrate and pass on as benefits to its customers and the community at large. Comparisons also allow organizations to identify gaps and emulate good examples for improvement.

A recurrent problem with benchmarking is that comparisons are complex and it may be difficult to find sufficient information about competitors to objectively compare end-to-end production, ending in a biased "tunnel vision".

Organizations can start building benchmarking strategies identifying customers' buying experience, recognizing needs that induce purchase of products and services and following up after purchases to identify factors that influence customers.

Quality-driven organizations conduct systematic benchmarking for the following important reasons: 1) to demonstrate to customers, potential customers, and the wider community objective quality standards that add value to products and services; and 2) to serve as a sustainable quality model for other organizations to emulate, fulfilling the organization's social responsibilities to contribute to improving the community.

Here are some questions for consideration in benchmarking assessment:

- How does the organization use its customers' knowledge to develop and improve benchmarking strategies?

- How does the organization assess innovation in benchmarking?

- How does the organization integrate horizontally with peer organizations to foster constructive competition to fulfill its social responsibility, helping its community?

- How does the organization project its sustainable quality principles and practices to peer organizations to strengthen the industry as a whole?

- How does the organization ensure it is a quality-driven example in the community?

Care of the environment (internal and external)

Quality-driven organizations pay close attention to environmental care inside and outside the physical structure. And although it may seem that the contribution of one organization can be limited, there is substantial evidence that the environmental footprint of every organization can add up to generate significant environmental impact that can be managed undertaking a variety of approaches:

- Increasing attention to physical fitness is leading to the development of new organizational and urban environments. How does the organization meets these demands?

- Advances in technology allow organizations to reduce part of their environmental footprint including connectivity and video-conferences to substitute for travel, and locating offices in energy-efficient buildings.

- Recycling is a general concern and a specific responsibility for individuals and organizations.

- Beyond ecological concerns of environmentalists, organizations are creating *quality green teams* deploying strategies in the internal and external environment such as systematic assessment of paper waste policies, trash disposal, recycling hubs, and others, which are required by legislative orders or voluntary organization policies.

- The development of green areas, inside and around the organization, such as the gardens and harvested walls seen in Figure 10.1, are flourishing worldwide, contributing to cleaner environments. These are more attractive for customers and employees, who can use green spaces to take breaks from stressful operations, finding peace of mind to relax, which in turn can contribute to increase performance and productivity.

FIGURE 10.1   Green walls in a restaurant on Alexander Platz in Berlin (top) and Detroit International Airport (bottom)

Source: Author

Assessment methods and instruments

In the OIR, the organization describes the system used in data collection and analysis, and the instruments used to assess performance improvement and identify areas of improvement in this management area.

Results

Show results obtained in the variables, processes, programs, plans, etc. included in the Assessment Elements of this Management Area.

Organization Improvement Report (OIR)

OIR: A GPS analogy

OIR is equivalent to a GPS (global positioning system) in terms of following a specific road to advance to quality standards. The difference is that while GPS offers a paved road to follow, the OIR is a practical guide for people who work in the organization to pave a road to continuous improvement and quality standards built from reliable sources and increasing the reliability of the assessment and the validity of the results.

OIR, like GPS, provides a starting point or a snapshot of the original location and both show progress along the way, providing timely information about road conditions, prevailing climates, and an unobstructed sight of the road ahead. When OIR is properly designed it delivers the same results.

OIR is built by people who work *in* and *for* the organization and it helps users across the organization develop critical assessment capabilities to optimize decision-making, communications, and transparency. The instrument allows everybody in the organization to get involved in the quality transformation and share responsibility for continuous improvement.

Furthermore, technology overcomes the limitations of previously segmented methods of data collection and reporting, facilitating integral coverage of the organization and the external environment in unprecedented ways. Updated IT also allows old information systems to be linked to new data collection methods, facilitating access and analysis of longitudinal data.

OIR development procedure and performance assessment

To develop an OIR effectively it is helpful to follow a proposed protocol:

- The executive level of the organization makes the decision to adopt the HCMxSQ model and informs all the people in the organization (from executives to cleaning personnel). The purpose of this communication strategy is to involve everybody in the quality transformation and induce participation based on goodwill and the collective benefits of quality standards, instead of conformity with executive norms and rules.

- Promote transparency and inform employees that while the quality transformation implies more work initially to systematize data collection, analysis, and assessment of performance improvement, in the long run it results in less work simplified by increased efficiency.

- Volunteer executives lead the quality transformation, calling for the formation of quality teams in divisions and departments across the organization.

- Quality teams are formed by at least seven members, each member responsible for collecting and inputting information on the variables and process chosen to be included in the 7 Management Areas and 35 Assessment Elements of the HCM SQ model.

  ○ Each Management Area leader can invite, involve, and obtain the support of as many reliable volunteers as desirable to collect data to feed into the OIR for analysis[1]

  ○ Quality teams in each division/department meet periodically (weekly in the initial stages) to assess progress and coordinate data inputs in OIR

  ○ Quality teams across the organization meet monthly to discuss actual improvement and new directions

- At the end of the first trimester, all members of the quality teams meet to assess the structure and strategies of the OIR in conformity with the organization's improvement objectives.

  ○ This first OIR is used as the *start* of the road to the sustainable quality transformation

  ○ The first OIR is used for comparison of performance process improvements guided by the five stages of the Sustainable Quality Cycle assigning corresponding point scores

---

1   This emphasis on volunteers is down to two factors. First, sustainable quality management initially requires a significant degree of commitment to personal improvement as a necessary condition to effectively deploy sustainable organizational improvement. Second, quality is contagious. We observe that volunteer members work harder and more efficiently than people who are assigned to this task and their rate of success rapidly attracts increasing numbers of volunteers to participate actively in the quality transformation.

Every three months the OIR is updated to assess organization improvement and identify new areas of improvement to emphasize during the next period.

The OIR needs to provide data to: 1) clearly identify *strengths* in variables associated with the 35 Assessment Elements; and 2) facilitate identification of *areas of improvement and the actions* and plans to follow to improve them. At the end of a 12-month period most organizations have mastered data collection and analytical methods, gaining a clear picture of progress coinciding with interpretation of the score attained. Organizations that reach over 750 points, which is equivalent to 75% of the organization's processes showing continuous improvement, indicate attainment of sustainable quality standards. As a corollary, this organization could feel confident that it is ready to compete for a National Quality Award program with a high probability of achieving this prestigious performance excellence recognition.

I finish my books on sustainable quality with a traditional message: Quality is a road. Not a destiny. And a reminder: although the road is without a doubt challenging and laborious, nothing can compare with the joy of attaining quality standards ... to continue traveling.

About the author

Maria-Teresa is economist, educator and entrepreneur. After a career in academia, she founded the Global Institute for Quality Education (GIQE) to respond to the challenges in achieving sustainable development based on quality standards and high performance across multi-sectors and aligned with demands of the economy and inclusive societies. She is a recognized human-centered efficiency innovator and program designer working with and training problem-solvers worldwide. She is international author and lecturer in Quality Management. The US Government has recognized Maria-Teresa Lepeley for her service to the Board of Examiners of the Baldrige National Quality Award (2001–2005) and she has been adviser to the National Quality Award Programs in Latin American countries.